THE **LOW END** OF HIGHER THINGS

THE
LOW END
OF
HIGHER THINGS

David Clewell

The University of Wisconsin Press

The University of Wisconsin Press
1930 Monroe Street
Madison, Wisconsin 53711

www.wisc.edu/wisconsinpress/

3 Henrietta Street
London WC2E 8LU, England

1   3   5   4   2

Printed in the United States of America

Text design by Carol Sawyer of Rose Design

Library of Congress Cataloging-in-Publication Data

Clewell, David, 1955–
The low end of higher things / David Clewell.
p. cm.
ISBN 0-299-18570-2 (hardcover : alk. paper)
ISBN 0-299-18574-5 (pbk. : alk. paper)
I. Title.
PS3553.L42 L69   2003
811'.54—dc21   2002152710

ACKNOWLEDGMENTS

Grateful acknowledgment is made to the editors of the following publications where many of these poems first appeared:

The Georgia Review: "Desperate Measures"; "Not to Mention Love: A Heart for Patricia"; "Our Own Devices"; "We've Been Sleeping Together All Week"; "Wrong Number after Midnight"

The Laurel Review: "The Magician's Assistant Dreams of One Day Coming Clean"

MARGIE/The American Journal of Poetry: "Criswell Predicts: Moon Landing or Not, the Usual Weekly Gathering of Friends at the Brown Derby—Los Angeles, July 20, 1969"; "My Father's Less-Than-Celebrated Feud with Orson Welles"

The Missouri Review: "Going Wrong in the House of Neptune"; "In 1962 Redemption Was in the Air"; "Make Way for the Men of Science"

Pivot: "All You Can Do: For Benjamin, Not Yet Born"

Poetry: "Enough"; "On the Eve of His Retirement, the Weight-Guesser Goes All Out"

River City: "The Collector"

River Styx: "Yes"

Third Coast: "Belongings"

5 AM: "Inside the *Eagle,* Waiting His Turn, Buzz Aldrin Can't Believe What He's Just Heard"

"CIA in Wonderland" and "Enough" appeared in *The Conspiracy Quartet* (Garlic Press, 1997).

"Jack Ruby Talks Business with the New Girl: November 21, 1963" was first published in *Jack Ruby's America* (Garlic Press, 2000).

for Patricia and Ben,
at the high end . . .

CONTENTS

IV. The World Doesn't End in New Jersey

Walking on water wasn't built in a day.
—JACK KEROUAC

I.

Nothing They Won't Think of Next

The whole world is about three drinks behind.

—HUMPHREY BOGART

On the Eve of His Retirement, the Weight-Guesser Goes All Out

for the Jersey Shore boardwalkers, c. 1975 . . . and for The Great Detecto himself

i.

In her fortuneteller's booth, Madame Starlight pretends
to traffic in some version of a future no one ever saw coming.
But she's just five minutes ahead, right past Momo the Monster,
this side of the Tilt-a-Whirl. She's not about to tell you anything
you don't already know. She'll be reading you cold,
and it's nothing personal: some *you've been unlucky in love*
topped off with *but not always,* and she can't lose. Even as we speak,
someone's paying way too much again to be that unbelievably
amazed by not nearly enough. You could do a whole lot better
yourself, no matter whose hand you suddenly were holding. Forget her.
Forget everything that comes after what I'm about to tell you:
the bumper cars, the ring toss, the inscrutable Wheel of Fortune.
Forget especially the Three Milk Bottles. You could throw at those
until you drop, never guessing your own strength.

> I'm risking my good name,
lifted straight from this scale—a precision instrument that really can
substantiate the one thing I'm here to say. Believe me: The Great Detecto
can't possibly crystallize a single wisp of the future. This is about you
and me right now, old-fashioned science and arithmetic in action,

and because you have to give me two pounds high or low, the target's
bigger than it seems: the bowler, trying to pick up the 5-pin, imagines
the fat middle of the pin itself, but his margin's actually the diameter
of the ball to either side. It's not that tough when you think about it
standing there alone like that.

ii.

Guessing any man's a snap. Like dragging Main Street on Saturday
at noon, no hands on the wheel. There's not one curve or hairpin turn
that needs negotiating. Women I approach from another direction
entirely. I make sure to come in low, some crazy airplane kind of guess
flying underneath the radar, so they'll be less inclined
to give themselves away by stepping onto the scale and proving once
and for all how far I can go wrong. Not for the ridiculously puny
stuffed animal they'd get to walk away with.

There's very little chance
in the equation. This is a one-shot game of skill, and I'm the only one
who can play. So whether or not I'm mostly on the one-dollar money,
there aren't people hanging around all night, showing off
or going broke, trying to impress what's left of their wives or
the up-for-grabs boardwalk girls. There's no trading up for anything
bigger, softer, better. There's no better luck next time.
This isn't some clown shouting insults like *Fat Head* or *Bag-of-Bones*
from his seat above that laughable tank of water, and you can buy
all the chances you need to drown him out with maybe just one lucky throw.

Lit up in this unrelenting neon hubba-hubba, it's no wonder
people can't help themselves. My job's to insist they are exactly
who they are—but only once. I'm the expert weighing in again,

telling them what that means in pounds, the surest measure I know
of the way a life accumulates. I say *this is how much of you*
matters tonight. I say *you've got absolutely nothing to be ashamed of,*
as if they'll truly feel more satisfaction in going away empty-handed.
And even when occasionally I miss my guess, whatever's stuffed
stays stuffed that way forever in their no-less-disappointed hands.
I've done the best I can do. They have at least that to carry with them.

But I've got to be honest: most nights I'm so good, it hurts.
Just ask Madame Starlight, lately unlucky in making her customary
small fortune. But not always: her future here looks more promising
without the predictably uninventive, killjoy likes of me.

iii.

I'm going to miss this crazy life on the edge
of the only world there is. Most of all, the ocean at my back
swelling, rising, cresting, curling on itself until it breaks—
that thunder in the surf drowning out another day's inconsequential
noise, over and over, thousands of pounds
of elemental grace under pressure. Next to that kind of power, anything
we have to say is a word scrawled fast in the sand, and we're gone.
And whatever's left behind is swallowed up, goes out to sea
for a while. Until it all comes crashing back in again, maybe changed
but no less broken. One more absurd picnic gone irretrievably to ruin.
Stare at the flotsam long enough, and it sure enough takes on
the unmistakable size and shape of just one person, wrecked
on grief's high tide, knocked headlong in the undertow of desire.
These are the ancient, barnacled sorrows that followed us
when we first bellied out of the water, grew legs, and walked away
upright, trying never to look back. There are those days

that get to us: we're down on our knees again, and here comes some wave
that's been building for so long that by now it's packing the weight
of the world, and that's what we'll be feeling. I'm afraid
that's how we'd put it, too, if only we had the wind.

                                        Right here
is where that's undeniably measured, for the next few hours
at least: breath by goddamn living breath. I'm sizing it up for everyone
in the blood, in the bone, in what passes finally for resolve
in the muscle of the jaw, in the neurons firing a few more desperate rounds
before the swinging door in the brain comes unhinged completely.
Brick by human brick, the weight of the world is so much more
than any watery figure of speech. It's easily as real
as your astonished face. It's anybody's guess, and I've always said
there's nothing to it. You give me a lifetime in either direction,
high or low, and I can't miss. Tonight your dollar's in good hands,
but tomorrow none of this is any of my business. Tomorrow, like it
or not, your guess is as good as mine.

Wrong Number after Midnight

When I pick up, the voice on the other end is already off
and running: *You were right, man, you were so*
incredibly right, and now I'm more than sorry I didn't believe you
when you claimed that the only way to keep their voices out of our heads
was by using heavy-duty aluminum foil, the kind
our own mothers were crazy for when it came to preparing leftovers
for their deep-freeze oblivion. You tried to tell me:
regular foil's too thin for making any kind of proper headgear—
a ponderous buffer-zone helmet, or something less obtrusive and more
stylish, say, a wave-deflecting beret. Next time I visit,
I'll be sure to bring enough of the extra-strength for us both.

And although this sounds like something I certainly might have suggested—
perhaps only to my closest friends, it's true—it happens
that I didn't, and finally he stops to worry up a whisper: *This isn't*
my friend Stuart, is it? And I say *No,* and he says *Oh my God,*
man, they've gone and gotten through to you, haven't they? As if
he's the one who can't believe what he's hearing, who's never felt so
disconnected, standing in the middle of whatever room he's renting
in his suddenly less-than-accommodating life. There's no way
he can appreciate how accidentally he's reached me, how sympathetic
I really am—the one other person who might think it's worth trying,
this last-ditch defense against the aliens or the in-laws or those
frightening late-night infomercial people.
                                    It's after midnight again,

when everything that comes along is that much harder to resist,
and where I've come to live, more often than I'd like,
just a single touch-tone button away, apparently, from the madhouse.
I'm so wide awake now in the dark, it's not funny, and there's nothing
left to say along the miles of open line, nothing to do but quietly lay down
the receiver in its cradle, take the long walk back to sleep. And if I make it
that far again tonight, you can be absolutely sure that's when
the Venusian scout-ships will be closing in, or Patricia's mother,
and somewhere Mr. Car Wax Guru will be setting a Chevrolet on fire
to the paid-off astonishment of his TV-studio audience—one more
brilliant lesson in the virtue of sheer resilience—and he'll swear
nothing else on Earth can stand up to that kind of heat.
But three of us, more or less, in our foil-wrapped, American-as-baked-
potato wisdom, will know better. There's me, my wrong-number friend, and
Stuart, wherever he is right now. May his meds make him unbreakable,
and doctors never talk him fully out of his half-baked, hard-won silence.
May his friends wait until morning before ringing through to him there.

And let the plans of the space people and our relatives and anyone else
who would come to us in our woozy sleep, on this night at least,
come to naught. May they be foiled, with any luck. And with our blessings
or our curses, foiled again. May it turn out they've been looking,
all along, for someone else. And if they find us instead, certifiable
wrong numbers, may they have to tell us exactly how sorry they are.
And for how much.
                        Given the crush of increasingly unstable particles
in the universe, it's no small thing: how surprisingly undisturbed
we actually are, how quiet it so often is on our end of the line.
And whenever we get to thinking that's OK, there's quite enough
still ringing in our ears for one more night or for a lifetime,
here comes another one of those voices out of nowhere, saying
in so many words we haven't heard anything yet.

The Neighbors Are on TV Again

When reporters go asking the obligatory neighbors about the latest guy
who got himself a rifle and a wrong idea and went off,
weighted down, to a crowded restaurant or forsaken clock tower
or a downtown office building where he rode from floor to floor,
firing and firing and firing until no one was left to unload on,
and he turned the gun on himself at last—sadly, always last
in the immutable order of such events—just this once
I'd really like to hear even one of those incredulous neighbors say
You know, I always thought he was way out there,
somewhere the busses don't ever run. But it's no surprise
this almost never makes its way into the comfort of our living rooms.

I'd settle for the smallest bit of self-satisfaction, some *have you seen*
the car he drives? But what never fails is another tired reprise
of that quiet-man-who-kept-to-himself routine. Because that's how
they usually think of themselves, and now it seems this is undeniably
their story, too—no matter the extremes that someone's gone to,
getting it told again.
                        What they're being asked, of course, is the usual
did-they-see-this-coming, could-something-have-been-done?
As if of course they should have known, but instead they've been caught
napping, roused unceremoniously out of their no-idea sleep.
At least a hundred times we've seen the rumpled man in the ball cap
who can't stop shaking his head. The woman standing under her porchlight,
holding a crying baby girl in her pale arms.

This isn't to make light
of whatever carnage this time darkens another day. This assuredly is not
to pardon or apologize, diminish or justify. It simply happens
there's no shortage of reasons why some people are bound to snap
like rubber bands stretched thin around stacks of overdue bills
or wear out like fan belts in the grueling summer heat. Let's say
it's a tumor, a bad haircut, a surprise layoff at Chrysler.
Or a lover walking away at high noon, refusing even to turn around
and draw the shaky gun with the *Goodbye* flag stuck in its mouth,
and *bang,* the sudden opening in the heart is no one's idea
of anything funny. With no light in the window come evening,
what's left, I'm sorry to say, is the dark that everyone's afraid of.
And whether the heart, after all its incessant and solitary burning,
eventually goes out like an exhausted light bulb in its socket
or like a furloughed sailor in his raucous cartoon night on the town,
there's sure to be some real bleeding through the walls before it's over.

Any one of us could wake up sobered by the fragile promise of another day
breaking outside the window—a punishment more cruel, I'm afraid,
than unusual. The sun already done with us,
rising like a hanging judge in a hurry for his lunch,
although he wouldn't have missed the stunned looks on our faces
for the world. And we have to take it on the lam, slipping out the door
before it slams shut, again, with us inside. Our only way out of this
may be to get into the goddamn car and drive, and the hell with everything
the neighbors will think to say later, until we're somewhere else
completely. How we wound up there, running on fumes—and whatever
we might have passed along the way—is, to our relief, more or less
an inscrutable blur of no one's business and anybody's guess.

And now that these neighbors have learned how one of their own
has come to no good end again, maybe they'll know better

what signs to look for, who'll be the next to spin out, taking off
into a day so long he won't be making it back home the same person,
ever. One by one it happens, and always in this order: at first
it's only Mr. What's-His-Name, gone haywire. But pretty soon,
there goes the neighborhood.
                              Surely they must have had their suspicions:
pot-luck supper no-show, carpool holdout, and always that light
burning in his late-night room at the top of the house.
But they lived so close to him, sometimes that's hard to say.
They're trying to articulate their dismay for the record—anything
they still can't believe, over and over. Until what happened out there
on this cumbersome day in the world is almost beyond them. And with luck,
by tomorrow they're nowhere to be found, for days or weeks or even years—
although I'm betting that's too gracious a reprieve for me to hope for.

In some other neighborhood, miles or years away from here,
there might be a young girl who can't remember much about herself
as a baby in her mother's arms, except that somehow she lived through it—
even those long nights no one could stop her crying once it started,
and for no good reason they could think of. She was once that inconsolably
alive. And when at last it's her turn to be asked what did she ever
really know about whoever's gone wrong and done it this time,
she'll grow quieter than she's ever been in her life, keeping to herself
this uneasy sense of exhilaration—the way her heart is even now
engaged, an unpredictable engine she can't help gunning. She has no idea
how far it will take her, but in her most invigorating dream
it's the dead of night, a straight shot out of town, and she can't wait
to see what it can do when she puts her foot to the ridiculously bloody floor.

Jack Ruby Talks Business with the New Girl: November 21, 1963

I will say this only once to you, I promise: business
is business. It's nothing personal. All business
is good business. You heard of selling the sizzle,
not the steak? Be sure you're only sizzle. Nothing but.
They're hungrier than that, they can beat it somewhere else.
I run this place so clean, some nights people hear it squeak.

Smile all you want, but no life stories, ever. I never knew
a smile that hurt, but keep your real name to yourself.
And when you hear whatever name you're going by tonight,
it's your turn to dance. And you dance. With class. Like
nobody's business. You make your entrance, hit your mark,
and get it done. And let's face it: the music
isn't much. But it's all yours. Do what you can.

And somebody thinks he knows how to soften you up with sweet
talk or a roll of bills, remember: you always know better.
This is no business to make that kind of mistake in.
Take it from me: you don't want to walk into anything
you can't talk your innocent-enough way out of.

And if there's trouble you didn't see coming, don't worry.
That's what I'll be out there looking for. I may be incognito,
just another hat in the crowd. But if you want to know the truth,

all you have to do is ask. You say *Jack* and I swear
I'll come through. Say the word, and some guy's good as dead.
He'll learn fast: guys like him are our business, and who we are

is really none of his. As long as you're working for me,
you're covered. Partners. No matter how it has to mostly seem.
Yeah, you're the one who's out there at point-blank range,
but I will never leave you twisting in the wind, whichever way
it's blowing that night, alone in any of this business.

CIA in Wonderland

And ye shall know the Truth and the Truth shall set you free.
　　—Biblical inscription on the wall of the main lobby at CIA
　　Headquarters, Langley, Virginia

i. The Ground Floor

This is before guru Leary, before the Fillmores
East and West. Before Harvard or Millbrook, acid's own
private academy. Before the Pranksters ever
set foot on the bus. Before Lucy In The Sky or the hundreds
of raucous tabloid headlines like GIRL, 5, EATS LSD
AND GOES ON RAMPAGE. Before Flower Power took
to the streets. Before Human Be-Ins. Before the Haight.

This is 1949, and the CIA is already going wild
just thinking about LSD; there are memos full of *the secret
that's going to unlock the Universe.* They're looking
for a key, let's give them that. But the Universe might be
a little much for them right now. This is about who knows
how many secrets. This is about choosing sides: someone's
got a Cold War to win. This much, finally, is about how
The Company works: a few human beings in the paranoia business
can accomplish more than any outright politics of hate.

And this leads to the clandestine 1950s birth of MK-ULTRA,
a secret-within-a-secret, the CIA's special hush-hush baby
cutting its crooked teeth on the best of everything
its cloak-and-dagger daddy can buy. These are the days
of chemical and biological abracadabra, and there must be
some magic they can do with this amazing stuff from Sandoz,
now that they've contracted for exclusive buying rights.
And so the CIA scientists get cracking.

                                    They're not in this
for the glory, for the sacrament, for the fleeting glimpse
into altered states of being. Russia's already one reality
too many, so they're testing what they've been made to believe
could be a weapon, if only they can find a reliable trigger.
They're studying pharmaceutical ballistics, making it up
as they go along, diagramming theoretically spectacular
trick shots *sure to break the will of enemy agents:*
the soundtrack from a cartoon training film playing over
and over in some projection room above them.

And the hell with any mystical doors of perception. Show them
a window of opportunity instead, no matter how fogged-up:
If LSD proves to be inefficacious as a truth drug,
we will consider its potential as anti-interrogation substance.
Under its spell, our agents might be impervious to questioning.
Pop a tab of acid while in the fabled *enemy hands,* and suddenly
it's a different cartoon—that's Tweety, wide-eyed in the dark
of Sylvester's furry clutches: *I tawt I taw a puddy tat!*

This research gets a lot sillier, a whole lot
scarier later on. For now it's still about exhilaration:

I did! I did taw a puddy tat! Or words to that effect:
One small suitcase full of LSD could unstring every man,
woman, and child in America. Either way, there's no denying
the sheer adrenaline surge that always comes with knowing
just enough to be dangerous. They can't seem to understand
what manner of beast they're swinging around by the tail.
They'd love to let go about now and walk away with their lives,
but we can see the obvious problem: they're already in
way over their cartoon heads, so far there's nothing
totally out of the question. Nothing they won't think of next.

ii. Physician, Heal Thyself . . . But Barber, Don't Try Cutting Your Own Hair

At first the CIA was interested only in willing participation. It was a decision with more swagger than humility in it: they would prepare for operational testing by taking the LSD themselves. And maybe it seemed like a good idea at the time: government agents on drugs they'd barely had a chance to imagine.

For weeks they took turns stirring it into their morning coffee. They tripped at the office, in the streets, at home. They fired off memos and service revolvers, drove spiffy convertibles, went shopping for ties. They ran zigzag on the beach and made whatever love they had left at the end of the day.

Sometimes they worked in pairs, and it was high school gym class all over again: one person somewhere on the ropes. The other person playing spotter, trying to look busy, hoping the coach will forget they're supposed to trade places when his partner comes down.

They observed, questioned, analyzed each other. They put in for overtime to make sense of their copious notes. By now the reasoning was monotonously simple: if they could *penetrate the Inner Self* and reach some kind of tenuous understanding, they would *know better how to manipulate a person—or how to keep him from being manipulated.*

One is known by The Company one keeps.

There were unmitigated disasters. But a few surprising triumphs, too. And which was which depended a lot on who was doing the talking.

■ ■ ■

What came through the closed door was the realization . . . the direct, total aware-
ness, from the inside . . . of Love as the primary and fundamental cosmic fact.
    —ALDOUS HUXLEY, DESCRIBING HIS FIRST LSD EXPERIENCE

I didn't want to leave it. I felt I would be going back to a place where I wouldn't be
able to hold onto this kind of beauty. . . . The people who wrote the report on me
said I had experienced depression, but they didn't understand why I felt so bad.
They thought I had had a bad trip.
    —CIA OPERATIVE, ON HIS OWN LSD EXPERIENCE

For me it seemed as if the sky itself was opening up, and every bit
of available light from whatever passes these close-fisted days for
heaven came pouring down. In no time I found myself made up entirely
of all the colors in the visible spectrum. I was Agent ROY G. BIV,
a grade school mnemonic come to life in the street, where everything
became its own rainbow, layer after layer of light so soft I was sure
nothing on Earth would ever break again. Sharp edges disappeared
in a flash, and people's hearts fluttered out of their cages,
flying through that Monet afternoon: faces of the picnickers,
cherry blossoms falling, the bridges over the grey Potomac
all suspended an eternity together in mid-air, in molecule
after woozy molecule of Monet's definition of light. This world
so suddenly absorbing whispered its first secret in my ear:
it existed side by side with the one I was outgrowing, a cheap
seersucker suit and white bucks I never wanted to be caught dead in.

And I was in love all over the place: with the woman in the bakery,
shimmering among the cruellers in her powdered sugar coat of light.
With the blind man working the newsstand, with his light touch,
with feeling he could somehow see exactly what I was seeing: yes,
we were surrounded by light, but we were also part of the light

around everything else—the ecstatic hum of morning traffic,
shopkeepers lowering their awnings, another day's auspicious signs.
I could have kissed the glowing head of Ike himself, but then
there would have been Nixon, waiting for his. And there's no light
in Nixon: black-and-white exception, hallucination without end. And still

I must have walked a dozen miles in convoluted love until I came to
a sad understanding: all this was bound to wear off completely, fade
like even the finest perfume and the woman who swore it would last
forever in the middle of someone's wildest dream.
I didn't want to turn the sorry corner where things would be colored
only one way or another for the rest of my official life—
briefings, contacts, passports, false I.D., a wife who's not allowed
to know me half as well as she might think: this year I'm in sales
and I have to travel. Believe me, there's no pleasure in explaining
every trip I take these days is someone else's business.

■ ■ ■

Today another agent took his turn. It's a joke around the office
coffee pot: *What would you like in that?* Just the thought of coffee
was enough to make him nervous, but he took the steaming cup from me
as if it were a ceremonial torch. Later he ran out of here like a man
on fire, and given his weeping and yelling, I'd have to say love
was the furthest thing from his mind. It was the only way he could tell
his side of the beguiling LSD story. I finally found him broken down,
trembling in a downtown fountain. He'd barely begun, and already
his face was washed-out, the moon reflected in water. In nothing flat
his code name was *Apple* to my *Orange*, our sadnesses that incomparable.

But the two of us were Company men in the service of our country,
and I wanted him to believe me when I held him in my arms:

we were in this together, no matter how far off I might have seemed,
I was on his side for now, for as long as it took him to make
his precarious way back to himself. Beyond that, I couldn't say.
He did most of the talking anyway, whispering his terrible secret
confusion in my ear: he wanted to die, no he didn't, and yes, please,
and he was going to make up his mind if it was the last thing he did
before he stepped out of that fountain hours later, dazed but renewed
or before he drew his gun like a different conclusion entirely.
The world behind his eyes was a hideous flower in bloom, and he
was going to pull off its petals, one by one, until he had his answer.

The crowd that had sprung up around us by then stood quietly,
not quite sure what they were seeing: old-fashioned slapstick or dedication
in action: two grown men in suits in a fountain, drenched and carrying on
in the line of duty, in the name of research. I wanted him to see it
my way, even for a minute, as if we had that kind of time forever
and we'd never be infiltrated again, compromised over and over
by the relentless white light of another day we really believed this time
would come over to our side after years of working against us,
spilling its colorful guts like sunlight when it hits the fountain's spray
exactly right. We wouldn't need any more coffee to keep us up all night
the rest of our lives.
                    Meanwhile, the laboratory boys have who-knows-
what in mind. They're still sweating out the fate of the Free World
if only we could see them already heading back to their drawing board,
trying to keep quiet about some new plan sure to save the day tomorrow:
No one's seen anything yet. But it's no secret what's coming
through the curtains in the morning. In spite of what we thought we saw
in the day before. That's what I'm afraid of. And I could have told them so.

iii. Frank Olson Is Flying

We do not target American citizens. The nation must to a degree take it on faith that we who lead the CIA are honorable men, devoted to the nation's service.
—RICHARD HELMS, FORMER CIA DIRECTOR

In 1953 at the Deep Creek Lodge in western Maryland—originally built as a Boy Scout camp twenty-five years earlier—the Agency threw a get-together for its Army friends on the cutting edge of biological warfare. We don't know what kinds of stories they told around the fire, but these guys were a long way from Boy Scouts. It was going to be a harum-scarum night, and they weren't always prepared:

Frank Olson—family man, lover of practical jokes, specialist in the air-borne delivery of disease—was handing out his trademark exploding cigars when the room started pinwheeling unbelievably around him. A kaleidoscope turning in his head. He'd had no more than his usual two fingers of Cointreau, so he figured it was someone's idea of fun, someone trying to kid the kingpin of kidders. He resorted to his favorite expression—*You guys are a bunch of thespians!*—his distinctive way of saying he was onto them now, the joke was over. But when a general cleared his throat and announced that certain guests had been slipped *a mind-altering chemical* as part of a *Classified experiment,* Olson wasn't laughing anymore.

It was all he could do to navigate the dark hallway back to his room. From out of his pockets he took his unused sticks of Onion Gum, his packets of Itching Powder. He unpinned his Squirting Carnation, his very own Purple Heart. He stared at his ridiculous arsenal of tricks and began a night of sobbing that wouldn't quit. He'd been caught in mid-sip with a version of the Fly-in-the-Ice-Cube, and it was too late now to spit it out. He felt like that guy in the drawing on the package, smoke and lightning coming out of his ears, his eyes popping out of his reddened cartoon face. It was hard to tell if he was angry, or embarrassed. And someone in the background, pointing and laughing. That always seemed to be an important part of the picture too.

When Olson somehow found his frazzled way home the next day, he barely spoke with his wife, Alice: *Wait until the kids go to bed and I'll talk to you.* But all he could manage out of his own bleariness even then: *I made a terrible mistake.* She tried to tease it out of him, or at least tease him out of his malaise. When she smiled her most provocative smile and called him *Mr. Secrets,* he informed her that whoever wasn't making fun of him was trying to destroy him. And suddenly, what choice did she have? She didn't know whether to laugh or to cry.

In the weeks that followed, his anxiety grew. He only wanted to sleep, but the thought of closing his eyes made him nervous. He couldn't even make it through the simplest grace before meals. Not that he felt much like eating. A bite or two was all he could ever choke down. He was nervous going out the door, nervous in his car, nervous all day at the office where the telephone on his desk was a bomb that could go off at any time.

And if Frank Olson was nervous, the CIA was nervous. If Olson was spinning further out of control, an accident waiting to happen, they had to be more than a little concerned about the inevitable pile-up behind him. They gave him the name of a doctor with Top Secret clearance in New York who worked with LSD under Agency contract. Maybe he could bring Olson around, back to his predictable, good-natured self.

And when it was Olson's turn to sign in with the waiting room receptionist, he couldn't help but notice the X-Ray Specs she was wearing. *What a bunch of thespians;* they'd been expecting him. He took out his most reliable pen and wrote his name in Disappearing Ink. By the time the nurse had prepared the Foot-Long Hypodermic Water Pistol, he was already gone. He'd decided: there was nothing anyone could do to change his mind.

▪ ▪ ▪

Frank Olson is flying, and if he ever stops
it's a long way down. He's thrown himself through
the drawn blinds, the closed window
of his tenth-floor room at the elegant Statler Hotel.
He's not thinking of terrible secrets, sweet revenge
or his footnoted place at the bottom of another page
of history. This begins his moratorium on thinking.
For weeks he's had nothing but bad ideas: poison
pen notes from his own secretary. The gas jockey's
small talk, some mockery in code. The Agency, dropping
a dime sure to lead to his imminent arrest. Everything
boiling down to the sticky, obvious residue of his undoing.

And so he'd show them all in the end
what he could still do: Frank Olson is flying high,
and if he ever stops, it won't be to reconsider
the voices that keep telling him to tear up his papers,
his money, to throw away his wallet, set fire to his clothes.
It's a long way down, and tonight the lights of 33rd Street
are burning for him: the smoke shop's got his favorite brand,
the all-night grocery if he's hungry, a tavern
where the regulars could make him feel right at home.
He's not the kind of guy to get out much, but tonight
is a different story: Frank Olson is flying
smack in the face of what will become the official
version of his dying: he will have jumped or maybe
fallen out of a window in New York because he suffered
from chronic ulcers. And it's someone else's turn

to worry now. Frank Olson is flying, and if he ever stops
someone will be working hard to make sure there's no

connection between a dead man and the CIA. Let alone
LSD. Someone will bring his widow the late-breaking news,
a bad dream in the middle of the night. And she'll wait
twenty-two years until she wakes up to what really happened,
a copy of the *Washington Post* at her door with its story
about years of illegal CIA domestic operations. And for her,
too, it's going to be a long way down. Finally she'll know

everything: Frank Olson—specialist in the airborne delivery
of things insidious and nearly invisible—is goddamn
flying. And if he ever stops, it's got to be
a long way down to the bottom, to the sickening thud
of a life falling apart this irretrievably. To the flashing
lights of the squad car and the spiritless chalk outline
of one more broken man on the sidewalk, all that's left
to represent him. It's crazy, what in the world
can push some people over the edge, the cop might say
to no one in particular. Certainly not to the widow Alice,
so many unsuspecting years away from the scene of the crime.

She'll have to think about it this way: her husband knew
exactly what he was doing, and he couldn't help himself.
In her better dream he's flying, no matter how desperately,
and she sees him firing up the trick cigar of his life,
right there before the lights go out. She only wishes
he could be here to watch it explode—this long after
it was handed over—in someone's fat, astonished face.
Yeah, that's real funny, Frank. I mean it this time. Funny.

Frank Olson is flying. And it's a long way down.

iv. Why It Almost Makes Sense

LSD. LBJ. FBI. CIA.

—LYRIC FROM *HAIR: THE AMERICAN TRIBAL LOVE-ROCK MUSICAL*

Because under the cover of slapstick, the more ridiculous
the better, our spooks were willing to try anything once
so easy to laugh at, to disavow if anyone ever went public:
telepathy, REM sleep-teaching, sensory deprivation,
hypnotically induced anxieties, tunnel vision, cluster headaches,
subliminal projection, aphrodisiacs, electroshock and psycho-
suggestive lobotomy, sneezing powders, stinkbombs, exploding
cigars, marijuana, heroin, speed, diarrhetics, laughing gas.
And could someone please tell them what's so funny about LSD?

Because it was still the Cold War, it was Frostbite Falls USA
and Moose & Squirrel could cut up all they wanted—as long
as they found some way to defuse the dastardly shtick
of Boris & Natasha, *dahlink*. Because Fred MacMurray was riding
high, the Absent-Minded Professor who discovered flying rubber.
And so what's next, after his souped-up jalopy, beyond the sheer
Flubber hijinks and yucks? Because the Company's still looking
for the flimsiest practical application: maybe a little LSD
in Castro's scuba-diving mouthpiece, some itching powder in his wetsuit
would be enough to drive him crazy, cause him to go down for good.
Because no one's coloring with a full box of crayons, no one's
staying inside the lines anymore. And this is the best
they've come up with so far at the Central *Intelligence* Agency.

Because finally LSD was a whisper away from people in the streets
and who knew what those unsuspecting idiots would do when it got there?

Because they were barely out of the narcotic dark of the Fifties. Because they'd dance and dance, but never give the spooks their cockeyed due: the linguistic invention of *tripping*. Because the Agency knew, LSD or no, the KGB demanded getting back to, the Mafia and the Kennedys and Castro again, LBJ and maybe Elvis, Vietnam's opium highway, another nickel's-worth of dictator to bury or embrace. Because what the hell, acid might yet work its confusing magic to CIA advantage if only they'd give up quietly, let it go. Because the world wasn't about to change overnight, why not: let the damn sunshine in.

II.

Almost Glowing
in the Dark

■ ■ ■

and what good does all the research of the Impressionists
   do them
when they never got the right person to stand near the tree
   when the sun sank . . .
      —FRANK O'HARA, "HAVING A COKE WITH YOU"

■ ■ ■

Not to Mention Love: A Heart for Patricia

Not one more figure of speech, I promise,
not here, under the pressing weight of centuries
of metaphors insisting on the heart's unbelievable resemblance
to anything else we know. One more could finally break it
irretrievably, and I don't want that kind of metaphorical blood
on my hands. So this time around, let the heart be the heart
the surgeon discovers when he lays open the chest so gently
it's easy to miss the self-effacing beauty of precision,
the way he comes at it directly, the only way he knows.
And the heart, exposed exactly for what it is: homelier
than we'd like to imagine. And alive beyond compare.
Here, the heart is the heart, and isn't
a fist or a flower or a smooth-running engine
and especially not one of those ragged valentines
someone's cut out, initialed, shot full of cartoon arrows:
the adolescent voodoo of desire. Here nothing's colored
that impossibly red.

                There's nothing cute about it. The heart
is the heart, chamber after chamber. Ventricular. Uncooked.
In all its sanguine glory. I couldn't make up a thing
like that. The heart's perfected its daily making do, the sucking
and pumping, its mindless work: sustaining a blood supply
that's got to go around a lifetime.
Sure, there's a brain somewhere, another planet

just seconds or light-years away, and maybe some far-flung
intelligence madly signalling for all it's worth—
but the heart wouldn't know about that. It has its own
evidence to go on. What's convincing to the heart
is only the heart. It doesn't have the luxury of stopping
to weigh, to reconsider, to fold and unfold the raw data of the world
until it's creased beyond recognition. Some days it can't distinguish
a single sad note from a chorus of exhilaration, but still
the heart has its one answer down to a science: *yes.* Over
and over, that iambic *uh-huh.* Whatever it takes, some kind of nerve
or unlikely grace: the heart never knows what to think.

     ■ ■ ■

If this poem has had its moments already
when I haven't been quite as good as my word—
when the heart's been anything less than the heart
or even the tiniest bit more—believe me, I've tried
hard to keep the heart in its proper place for once. It's not
in my mouth or on my sleeve or winging its way lightheartedly
in circles over my head. It's more or less right
where it belongs inside me, no small thing. And not to mention love
even once by its own name, Patricia:
that's a proposition I never meant to enter into, anywhere.

So when you turn out the light
and this page goes as dark as the room you're lying down in
and for one night at least there are no more distractions,
it's my heart you'll be listening to. And it's yours.
We fit together so well sometimes it's not easy
telling whose lips, whose arms, whose heat in the groin,
whose very good idea. I'm not taking any chances

bigger than the one you've given me—your insistent heart
mixed up with mine: *uh-huh, uh-huh, uh-huh,*
and my heart has never been the heart it is right now.
It's what we've both been waiting for: I'm asking you
to make of it what you surely will, to take it from here,
in your love beyond these imperfect words, please
take it wherever you're going tonight from here.

Our Own Devices

i.

As a kid I never thought about how much I was asking
for disappointment when I sent away for anything in the mail.
I spent too many days in a row hoping this time would be
different. It took me a while more than childhood
to finally get the idea: nothing ever
really arrives on time, full enough of its advertised wonder.
Not the government-surplus weather balloon, sagging badly
in front of my unamazed friends. Not the Lift-All (or, apparently,
Nothing-At-All) Magnet. Not Ventrillo, the throw-your-voice gimmick,
its *lemme out* exclamation floating, word-ballooned, above a trunk
some sweating, skinny guy's been shouldering the weight of
all his cartoon life. I wanted that *lemme out!* to be mine, the momentary
power to relocate anywhere I couldn't possibly be. Oh: and definitely
not the Sea Monkeys.
                            So little in the far-flung world managed to live
up to my inflated-beyond-all-realistic expectations, it's no wonder
I went eventually soft, easier to please. Consider the Yogi Bear Mask
I ordered from Kellogg's in 1961—the one time I was burned completely
past any postal recognition: no mask, no refund, no sugar-frosted word.
If it were to show up here today, I'd have to take it
on faith that never would have occurred to me when I was small:
on its own terms, no questions asked. A cardboard miracle.

ii.

Ever since you and I made it all the way through
that catalogue *For Loving Couples,* went far enough past modesty
to put our mostly unmitigated order in the mail,
I'll admit it—I'm a little nervous, I'm that little
child who's never lost heart: the familiar dizziness, the height
of anticipation. He's letting his hopes go sky-high again.

So if you could keep holding onto my hand and tell me, as calmly
as possible: did we really ask for Mr. Missile (*ready to explore
every part of the galaxy*), for The Ladyfinger (*so small it can fit
in your purse, pleasure you anywhere without detection*)? Did we stop
at the hot-pink Jelli-Master and consider the ramifications
of *friendly, hygienic vinyl?* The promise of Thunder Balls, let alone
the built-in swagger of the Vibro-Thunder variation?
When we got to The Juicer, The Moon Man, the regal bearing
of Sir Knobby, we forgot all about the virtuous Little Something
and flipped back to Mr. Big Shot (*because you work hard, you play
even harder*). But tell me, if you can, that our heads stopped spinning
before we sprang for the *great and powerful* Love Cage—we could never
afford the batteries. Surely by then we must have had the unsettling
feeling that we weren't in Kansas anymore.

iii.

Every day that the mailman comes and goes in his usual
blue hurry, we understand all too well: it's nothing personal again.
I don't know if I'm relieved or disappointed. No creams, no lotions,
no sprays, oils, or powders. Nothing the least bit *Confidential*

with our names unabashedly on it. I don't have to tell you:
part of me can't wait. Even Lee Harvey Oswald must have smiled
that day his fifteen-dollar mail order rifle finally arrived. Part of him
had to know he was in way over his head, but no one's yet proved
to our satisfaction that he actually pulled the trigger, right?
Who would suspect the likes of us? Our motives have always been pure
whimsy, most of the time. In the privacy of our own home.

It looks like another night we'll be left to our own devices.
We have our sturdy, unmade bed to fall back on, as if to say
we've always been this easy, the most consenting of adults. We'll carry on
with whatever we've got in our own exotic inventory of unbridled love:
there's Tossing the Salad, The Jumper Cables, Godzilla vs.
the Spanish Fly. The seldom-seen Yogi Picnics in Jellystone Park. Elvis
at the Gates of Graceland. It's not hard to believe that we've come
to this: between us, we can get away with anything.
So let's throw the motor into *High,* kick back and loosen up
the sweet restraints of our discretion. Right now there's no harnessing
what we've got for each other, bad. Satisfaction guaranteed, or
whatever's left of our good names back. Our money, not quite
as well-spent as we'll be tonight—and anything that's coming
in the mail tomorrow will be just what we've always wanted.

Second Wind

i.

It seemed like such a good idea, growing up:
if I had to walk my family's narrow hallways, I'd find a room
amenable enough to be myself in, find words they couldn't
bring themselves to say. Words that might have something to do
with the life I dreamed of getting away with out the door,
one day, forever. I scribbled hard into so many nights,
writing myself into any world where sooner or later I belonged.
I made it up as I went along, and when it turned into *Zombies
from Zomboolia,* I stapled those pages between two pieces of grey
cardboard from my father's pressed white shirts. I'd show them:
a limited edition of one. I couldn't believe how long it took
to get it down just right, a tale that positively meant
everything to me when I was nine, and for the life of me now
I can't recall a single thing that happened. You know: that old story.

The first night that Poetry came to me, licking its painted lips,
lying through its metaphorical teeth when it said *Come on,
I'm easy,* I fell hard for every guarantee: similes like
open windows. Luxuriant images without end. Solace of a music
as effortless as breathing. All the sweet nothings I could handle
with Poetry's startling tongue in my ear. It was something
like love, another chance, and I took it, never dreaming
how fitful it would be, how many nights I'd give it everything I had

only to wake up completely in the dark again. I had no idea
I'd spend untold years trying to put a life into any words
that possibly could save it for a minute, suggest a discernible shape
and weight enough to matter, keep it from collapsing entirely
in the static: the white noise of one more day going off the air.

You stumbled on a small, imperfect miracle in me: I'm talking
some threadbare antechamber of the heart that refused to go under,
lit up like a diner in a run-down neighborhood, Open All Night
all those years for no good reason. And that's where you came in,
apparently, for good: a thousand cups of coffee later,
you're still unmistakably here every morning for breakfast.

ii.

There must be a hundred poems I know most of, but
I can't make it through any of them before going wrong
at least once. *Adam / had 'em* doesn't count. I wish
I could say a few of the bigger things by heart: *Out of the Cradle,
Endlessly Rocking. Asphodel, That Greeny Flower.* Actually I'd settle
for casting a shorter spell: say, *The River Merchant's Wife.*
I can't get these poems totally out of my head, and by this time
I should know better: when it comes to getting anything I love
exactly right in words, I'm usually found wanting.

That's when I dummy up and turn
to the shadowy place on your neck, that thrill in the quiet
small of your back. I'm learning to go on sheer rhapsodic nerve,
poetry's ridiculous bravado. I'm going back to school
in the basics of everything that's gone without saying:

how luminous moments accumulate, how we are the connecting
lines between them, by now so many constellations waiting to be named.

I've wasted whole days thinking nothing but the perfect word
would do, but lately what comes over me sometimes
is the absolute bliss of silence, and I want to stay up all night
with you in the middle of my life.

iii.

If by any chance there's been the slightest whisper of grace
in any line I've ever written, I assure you it's not much
compared to how you stretch out, luxurious in your strawberry bath
when you think I'm not watching.

iv.

These days when all is said, but not quite done, not nearly,
we're just getting started.
When the typewriter insists on humming, dumbfounded, into the night,
when the dictionary's patience wears thin as paper before running out,
when every inkling of language itself is exhausted,
love's our second wind—a breeze through the open window
murmuring shy in the curtains, finally rustling the sheets
with its soft sighing. And try as we might, we simply can't say
enough about that kind of love.

                    You're the one saving my prosaic life
one lung-emptying breath at a time. And any words that come

out of that naked, elemental heat are primal, one-celled, nothing
for the ages: the oldest death-defying music known.

v.

You've been working on your own rough drafts for so long
it's hard to remember any other life. That's how it is with us:
we've always wanted the world in writing—not because otherwise
it can't be trusted, but because some days it's way too easy to believe.

When we were younger, none of our words were really meant
to save the fledgling likes of us completely.
They were there to keep us going until at last we came across
those words that spelled out our best idea yet: *each other.*
What we've never been at a loss for, since.

                                   And when poetry happens
to whisper in our ears, this time we'll be ready: we'll understand
with pleasure it's nothing we have to get away with anymore.
This is our life together, so far beyond words that we've almost
caught up to them again. For all the good they'll do us.

For too long we had a lot to account for in someone else's version
of the world. Now, where we live for poems and they come
or they don't for days, weeks, even months at a time,
no further explanation's necessary: we're each other's alibi
for life. Either way, we don't have to feel guilty, but maybe we should
let the local authorities know we're here. Let's tell old Ezra
we are the news that stays news, tell the well-meaning doctor
no ideas but in bed. Together we've found the perfect marriage

of form and content. At least a thousand variations later
on the promise of *I do,* we still read each other
loud and clear.

       And when I sing myself in you—
the multitudes and contradictions in this boisterous swirl of atoms
hanging tough and slowly, painstakingly assuming the shape of a man
who never guessed he'd bring himself to love quite like this—
something tells me my heart will never stop
breaking wide open: it's you every time, singing back.

All You Can Do: For Benjamin, Not Yet Born

You are something we said last year, and more: you're what came
between us, what we did—our best idea yet.
By now you've done almost everything you can think of,
standing on your head in the amniotic dark. You've gone
nearly as far as physics will allow, an echo made flesh
across space and time, flexing your muscle, throwing
your burgeoning weight around in the oldest ocean known.

I've felt you kicking at the limits of the only world you've got,
ripples growing stronger in the long dark, the luxuriant bed
your mother's made for us both. And I can't wait
to see your face, your headfirst plunge into daylight.
I'll take you still kicking, drawing that first unmitigated breath
and screaming yourself some otherworldly shade of red—
that age-old declaration handed down in the quickening blood
on fire with this new life: forgive me for saying it this way, but
from now on it's every man for himself.

You are your wide-eyed parents somewhere way out here
writ small, already knowing better: making it up as you go along
on sheer impulse. You're all nerve and uncluttered heart.
You'll come soon enough to those overwrought first words
for what your life's been like so far: the fine-tuned mechanics
of crying and feeding and falling asleep and finally
crawling into a day so enormous, you'll think it never ends.

But under your own power at last, your tiny kingdom come.
Sometimes it will be all you can do to smile that ridiculous smile.
It's a wonder anything gets done, here on Earth as it is.

And we'll be right with you, on our knees
in your extreme of gravity—humbled or grateful or utterly
exhausted just imagining the act of standing up
and wobbling, trying to get anywhere with those erratic baby steps
before the inevitable crash-landing on a planet that thinks nothing
of spinning us off balance for the hell of it.
                                        Thanks to you
and your small brilliance on the horizon, we can already make out
voices in the distance, singing the restless everywhere to sleep
and waking them later, still a far cry from anything they dreamed.
There's no mistaking the discombobulated joy, the death-defying
acrobatics of walking into the rest of our lives from here.

The Collector

i.

After putting in a full eight hours and coming up short
in towns where I'd found success on previous flea-market Saturdays—
not a single blue manifestation of Charlie the Tuna
in his elusive plastic glory, no telltale Reddy Kilowatt zigzag
embodiment of energy in action, no electricity in the air, no cool
so-bad-they're-good ceramic beatnik Daddios, no yellowing
Krazy Kat or *Pogo* in their threadbare Sunday funnies best,
no worn-out-of-this-world copy of *Those Sexy Saucer People,* discarded
for not exactly living up to its complicated front-cover promise, no
promising anything that needed my saving for the rest of the day or for good—
I walked oddly unencumbered through the twilight parking lot with my son
who, in his ancient four-year-old's wisdom that comes from living a life
much closer to the ground, seized on an empty box of Good & Plenty
and made his trademark declaration: *I collect these, you know.*
He arrives at decisions like that in an instant, and unfailingly
they become him, until there's no going back to whoever he was before.

And my part was, as always, to carry it home, safe in my pocket—
the driver, the courier, the muscle, the mule—to smuggle it inviolate
across some invisible border to where it absolutely matters again.
His is not the standard collector's zeal, some nearly impossible quest
for completeness, the one missing piece by now larger than life,
where condition, they say, is everything.

It's nothing he'll spend whole days or nights or years on,
curatorially speaking. This is about a more haphazard accrual,
a steady accumulation with no discernible shape, save
that it's so easily accommodated in his wide-open mind's eye:
You know I need this for my sculpture that never ends.

His pursuit is effortless, a masterpiece of circumstance
and sheer improvisation, like Coltrane at the Village Vanguard
picking up a tune of no particular note and blowing it
inside out—the fiercest declaration on record of *My Favorite Things.*
My son knows by heart how that one goes. Every day
he's that alive, working on another small piece of his world:
counting it off, already dressed and hurrying through breakfast,
looking to come in so true and so sure that this time it will stay played,
his way, forever. He's got the chops already for the solo of a lifetime.
Even now he's stretching out, making it up and laying it down
as he goes along, riff by breathless riff.
                                             And surely
his best guesses are as good as any in the one museum display
he can't get enough of: skeletons of ghost-white bones made up to look like
dinosaurs, those staggering creatures we're actually supposed to believe
once walked the Earth, this way or that, until something even bigger
that no one can agree on came along from out of nowhere,
and there was no way they could save their suddenly puny selves.
The museum calls this a highlight of its Permanent Collection, but
no matter how skillful the arrangement, how aesthetically pleasing,
always what's missing is a certain assurance that says *this
really counted,* once, for something. We need to witness
the weight of conviction fleshed out before our eyes, some bleeding
beyond the bare-bones recollection of an earlier place or self or
catastrophic season that, at last, isn't otherwise humanly possible.

ii.

Here, on his small red table in the living room tonight:
a pine cone, a feather, a scrap of aluminum foil, a key
a long way from whatever it opens, a row of mismatched buttons.
When he says *I belong to them*, I know they mean the world.
And he is there for them, for keeps. Even now
on his long way into sleep, he knows every one of his secret pleasures
is safe with me. There's never a day he walks away from, empty-handed.

Sometimes that kind of power falls into the wrong hands: folks who can't ever
have enough Hummel figurines or angels or Elvis-on-black-velvet. And what,
exactly, are those salt-and-pepper-shaker people thinking? Leigh Hunt spent
a lifetime assembling his album of famous human hair, but he was one of those
hopeless Romantics, and should be pardoned accordingly. My fellow flea-marketeer
Ernie, world-renowned sculptor, unloaded his trove of kitschy 1950s
Space-Age lamps on me: *Can you believe I'm now collecting celebrity shoes?*
This was years ago, and I believed him because I wanted to believe
anyone can always make room for a few more needs of his own choosing.
Because sooner or later there's world enough we have too little say in.
Because we're better off knowing the name of anything we're not looking for.

Between my son and the woman who bore him, who bears up herself so gracefully
under the weight of whatever her boys are lugging home these days,
I have so much already. But I'll be setting my Charlie the Tuna
alarm clock for us all because I still want days like tomorrow,
when Ben will wake up, running full-tilt again into living-room daylight
illuminating his small share of the planet he laid out on display
so carefully the night before. Believe me, no one could be any more delighted
that it's still, all of it, there. And when he looks down from the unassuming
height of his young powers at what he's managed to make of his life so far,

he will see that it is good. And there is plenty
more, he'd like everyone to know, where this came from.

We've Been Sleeping Together All Week

because we're too exhausted to make love. And we don't get it:
we thought by now the entire planet would be thrown off its precarious
balance, or wobble on its axis maybe just enough for someone else
to feel the slightest difference.

But the trains seem no less on time
pulling in, unloading, heading out again with tomorrow's fragile cargo.
The clerk at the neighborhood 7-Eleven is no more dumbfounded than ever.
Nights continue to swell with the usual sirens and alarms
and the same dogs all over town start up their shaggy doo-wop chorus,
as if no emergency could be greater than their need to be part of it, too.
As always the crew at All-Nite Donuts, sticky with jellies and creams,
can't wait for daylight to come.

Our refrigerator's still humming
with everything it's got, and we're somehow still adults: anything,
anytime we want. Whether it's good for us, or not.
And all we have to do is stay awake to get it. But between you and me—
and a four-year-old, sky-high on these longest days of summer
lighting up his face, quickening his blood, whose heart's not much
of a hiding place for anything right now, who truly could use another
glass of cold water, having gone dry again describing everything that happens
under the sun of his tiny kingdom, on his daily way to outlasting us
forever—that isn't always easy. We've made our bed, and we're not really
sorry, even now while we're lying in it, more or less married
to the pure physics of inertia: bodies at rest will tend to remain that way.

Sure, other lovers are trying to make up for the worn-out likes of us.
They're doing it the best they can in city parks, in hotel rooms,
on elegant drawing-room settees, even in the elfin grottoes
we've lately resorted to dreaming. And while I'm thinking *good for them,*
it isn't nearly good enough for me. Not when I need you
over, under, wrapped around, beside me in the world, the secret
places of your body laid bare and unforgettable.

By the time we fall back into the waking world again, our own son's
been up for hours, steeping himself in the mysteries of the indefatigable
Mr. Coffee. He brings us whatever he's figured out so far, one nearly
impossible cup at a time, as if this will be enough for us to make it
through one more of his overflowing days. After all, he's made it
his small, exacting business to live where nothing's out of the question.
So maybe we'll get unbelievably lucky:

                                        there's heavy breathing in the air,
but Ben's the only one asleep. And here's the plan: I'll be the one
asking some easy question over and over, my hand a whisper moving down
to the small of your back and into that last dangerous curve. You can be
the one with the answer undeniably right on the tip of your tongue.
We'll call this our private emergency.
And whenever we get even that far again, we can only hope
those restless dogs are down for the night, and they're not about to
wake our surprisingly dog-tired boy—who still can leave any dream
on short notice, who can talk himself unerringly through a whole
unlighted house. It's a cinch he'd find us huddled together, barely
able to contain ourselves, taking cover in the southwest corner
of the bedroom. We'd be almost glowing in the dark.

Yes

It must have been that story on the late-night TV news
about the guy they caught on tape who said he'd gladly pay
ten-thousand dollars to get rid of his wife, no questions asked,
if whoever's on the other end of the phone knows what he means,
that got you wondering out loud on your way to sleep, *But you still
love me, right?* I should have smiled or somehow sighed dreamily
or shot back the same question, lovingly, to you,

but my head was reeling with ten-car pile-ups, drive-by shootings,
Ebola, E. coli, hostage situations, the latest computer virus,
armies on the march in some burgeoning, far-flung country,
smart-bombs, dumb-luck Republicans, and mad cow disease—more
than anyone's daily minimum requirement of vicarious suffering
and indifference. I suspected your question wasn't merely
rhetorical, that probably you were counting on a fast, enthusiastic
yes, which was exactly the answer I had in mind at last

when the weatherman appeared with his arsenal of maps, numerical
mumbo jumbo, and the usual grandiloquent, weather-related gestures.
For all that, the weather takes longer than ever
to arrive with anything we can use, but at least no one's dead
of meteorological causes tonight in his world, where disasters are only
natural. When he says we're sitting under a dome of high pressure,
he means that only in his weathermanly way:

it's a good thing for us, and he'll be back with our forecast
in just a moment.

Meanwhile, I'm wondering if that guy on the phone
really would have shelled out more than they'd spent on the wedding
because maybe he was counting on some big insurance money, more than
enough to show the formidable redhead he sees each week in Payroll
she could be the new Mrs. Yahoo now, if only she'd stop pretending
men like him don't even exist. From the little I know, and none of that
from experience, it almost never works.

And suddenly I understand
your question. On another night, it could have been mine—so simple,
yes, the single thing none of us can honestly stop asking ourselves
about whoever's nestled so tightly inside those naturally percussive
chambers of the heart that we can't help feeling
even the faintest, inadvertent slight or slightest hammer-pressure
might be enough to set some volatile charge in motion, and then what
do we do about the gaping hole in the roof when the rain comes, finally,
pouring down? *Yes,* no wonder the small voice best kept inside,
that means nothing, really, and so much at once, sometimes gets out—
not because anyone's looking for trouble, but how about just a touch
of harmless reassurance that *yes,* we truly are in this preposterous world
together, still in this sturdy bed, on the same reliable side of love.

Now the weatherman's back with all we've been waiting to hear:
yes, what it's going to be like where we live, for the next five days
at least, as far as he can tell, and when he calls it weather to die for,
he's saying there's no way we won't love tomorrow,
whatever's headed in our direction next. *Yes,* I could have told you
that much, and should have, gladly, before you drifted off beside me
without an answer, and I'm left talking to myself and the sports guy,
who always knows a winning team when he sees one—although it's true
he has the luxury of a teleprompter and his own fat stack of notes.

If this last half-hour had been secretly recorded, you'd hear
the grey-white noise of those stories I got lost in, and then
after the overblown weather, finally a voice—grateful or relieved
or a little embarrassed—*more than sometimes I can say.*
I'd have the authorities play it over and over until you were sure,
when you woke up in the morning: that was, unquestionably, me.

I Keep Dreaming I'm on the Wrong Train, but I'm Still on the Right Track with You

It's always past midnight when it occurs to me
that once again I've blundered onto the Serious Business Express,
and I'm surrounded by people who could have been home hours ago,
but instead they're all still sitting here, taking it
seriously out to the boondocks, to the absolute end of the line
where they're bound to be shown the door unceremoniously, stranded
again in the middle of their lives, and there will be no taking it back.
But for the moment, they seem inexplicably happy to be here together,
riding into the same dark nowhere they've always been getting, and fast.
They're suitably dressed for the part in their Smiley Face neckties
and cell phones and laptops, their Countdown-to-2000 digital watches.
Surely they have some idea how late it is right now, but they can't stop
themselves from checking their e-mail one more time. They're so available
to the rest of the world, it's frightening. They're actually still
expecting another day's instructions.
                          And I'm afraid
I'm exactly what they've suspected for a while—a heathen
in their down-to-business midst, along for the strange ride, it's true,
but I'm on this train only by accident, some chemical spill
in my sleeping brain that needs attending to. Blame it on my less-than-
conscious, end-of-the-millennium nerves, but finally I'm incredibly tired
of hearing about the 21st century as if it's a hot-wired luxury
car just waiting to accommodate us all in our unprecedented getaway.
These folks could use a dose of big-shot prophet Nostradamus,

whose inscrutable, 16th-century quatrains are supposedly full of everything
he saw for us—pestilence, natural disasters. Untold miseries. And yet
somehow he managed to miss the commuter train completely.

My resumé says it all for me—I really should be somewhere
in the Serious Trouble club car, in my outmoded, unrepentant cups:
I'm happiest in the breakdown lane of the information superhighway—
hazards flashing, muffler shot, no acceleration to speak of—
humming behind the tiny wheel of my portable Smith Corona.
I have never interfaced, networked, or prioritized. I've never been
impacted. I have no box to think outside of. No address in cyberspace.
I've never knowingly closed a deal, taken a meeting, or done lunch—
although, make no mistake, I've had lunches done to me,
but my most rewarding lunch was far from work: a dressed-to-kill
cheeseburger with James "The Amazing" Randi, who showed me up close, once
and for all, exactly how the so-called psychics bend those easy spoons.
Now I'm an older dog than ever, with no time for New Age tricks.
I won't read *Auras Around the Office* or *The Stock Market, Chakras, and You.*
I'm not the put-your-positive-energy-to-work-for-you type, and I'll be sorry
if it turns out there's a parallel, toy universe next door
that's been running on batteries forever.
                                    My surest reference
is my second-grade teacher, who saw it all clearly enough for me
without calling on the extrasensory: *David doesn't work well with others.*

And the man next to me is suddenly talking
mutual funds, 401(k), CDs and Euro-dollars, which I hear somehow
as *Sonny Rollins. Mr. Tenor Madness himself,* I say, and I love out loud
that he's still blowing away the young technicians-only of the horn
until it's obvious in this guy's blank face that Sonny Rollins CDs
mean nothing to him. I'm just that desperate to catch on, to jump in,
punch-drunk in my little corner of the far-flung workaday world.

And now he's the one trying too hard. He's going to show me
he's a music lover too, and without warning or apology he's bursting
into shreds of pop tunes from the Seventies like *Kung Fu Fighting,*
Rhinestone Cowboy, even *Bad, Bad Leroy Brown* in a voice that's a cross
between Elvis and Richard Nixon, and either way I've got that *he's alive*
cold sweat going, and this much must be true: there really are alien beings
abducting some of us for their insidious hybrid experimentation,
and since I'm decidedly asleep, in bed somewhere, and that's apparently
how they seem to like to us, where on Earth are they when I need them?
Isn't my call important to them? I get at least that much
recorded assurance every waking day of my fragile commerce in the world.
So pick up, please. Pick up before another pathetic decade gets sung
to smithereens, and he stops just long enough to ask what business am I in
and in my best cartoon broker's voice I try to tell him *futures*—
any versions I can actually lay my hands on—but I'm stuttering like
Porky Pig on the market floor, and he hears a *few-few-few-few*
and might think I'm a fellow go-getter and not at all like my Uncle Bud,
whom my aunt used to call a real no-getter when it came to work,
which Uncle Bud almost never did. Bud's one-size-fits-all response
on occasions like this one consisted of his being *between situations,*
and he drank his way through the daily blur of want ads, convinced
he'd recognize his dream job if he ever found it.
                                        And this train ride
may be only a dream, but even my uncle, no matter how lost in his own
TV cop-show dream, would have to admit we've got a real situation here.

Outside the train window, dawn finally is breaking all around us
and the guy next to me's insisting there's nothing we can do to fix it.
I tell him I'll be right back but, chances are, I won't.
I'm excusing myself for the last time tonight, I'm taking off
for everything my cockeyed life is worth, making tracks for the open door.
I may be running late again, but rest assured, I'm running.

I've spent too many nights on this ridiculous train
full of the wrong kind of serious people and, seriously, I was thinking

of you. In my bag are a few more pieces of earlier days that needed saving:
tracts from the old-time flying saucer disciples, a Charlie the Tuna
transistor radio, an authentic swatch of the black-cloth night sky
that starred in *Plan 9 from Outer Space.* You may shake your head and smile,
even ask me do I have any idea how the first eight plans came to nothing,
but you're the only one who can see how I mean business, and as usual
you'll find a place for my far-fetched holdings in the expansive chambers
of your heart.
            Right now you're whispering my name from somewhere
on the other side of the waking world, wondering where I've been all night
beside you, and I can't wait to meet you halfway again in the long bed
of our life together and tell you—and there goes the rest of the millennium.
Here's Plan 10: I'll bring the coffee, you come as you are—so much stronger
than I am, even with coffee, without you. It's my kind of 21st century already.
If I've been talking in my sleep, I hope you'll understand. We speak
exactly the same broken language, so much of it just to say
it's never quite the same dream twice—I have never been in this much
love before. And if you think by now you've heard everything, all I can say
is in your dreams. You've got another thing coming.

This is the part where I should be feeling at least a little sorry
for the guy I dreamed up, pitiful songs and all, to sit beside me,
and now that I've given him the slip, what's he supposed to think about
civility and honor and where the human race so stuck on itself is headed?
May an answer come to ease his pain in one of those mind-numbing choruses
that, for no good reason he can think of, he's been attached to lately:
been through the desert on a horse with no name. And he'd feel good
getting off this train. I really should go back and apologize

to everyone who bought into this train anywhere along the line.
I wish I could honestly say I've done them wrong on this train again,
that next time, maybe, I'll stick around a little longer, I'll make this
easier to take for all of us. But I can't. This is where I get off
loving you.

III.

What We Got Away With

Your wig steers the gig.
—LORD BUCKLEY, ON FOUNDING
THE CHURCH OF THE LIVING SWING

Desperate Measures

Charles Bolton, aka Black Bart, robbed twenty-eight Wells Fargo stagecoaches, often leaving a taunting verse in the plundered strongbox. Upon his release from San Quentin, he assured the warden that his life of crime was over. Asked if he was still going to write poetry, Bolton said, I repeat, sir. I am through with my life of crime.
—FROM "BLACK BART, SHOTGUN POET"

Part of me feels really bad about this, but it's too late—
there's no turning back now. Here comes another no-account poem
that someone with nothing to lose is waving in your face, and it's time
to reach for the blue sky again. Sadly, there's no way of knowing
if the poem is actually loaded or not. It could be just a bar of soap
carved into the plausible shape of a poem, or a dimestore water pistol
knockoff of the real thing—although history doesn't seem to favor
jumping to those reckless conclusions. I say
better to play it safe. No one's going to get hurt today
if you listen carefully. Remember the cardinal rule the boss recited
on your first night of clerking at the Gas & Go: *There's no arguing*
with a poem. It's too easy to get messed up, and for what,
when you get right down to it? Give the guy with the poem
anything he asks for.
                        Whatever you do, please don't misunderstand
what this is all about. I want the full attention of your life
right up to this nerve-wracking moment. Give me everything you've got.
Don't be caught dead on the business end of an extended metaphor.

This is what happens when an unwitting public crosses over
into literature's high-crime neighborhood, although I'm guessing
you have at least some popgun verse of your own, holstered
conveniently within reach. These days, who isn't packing a version
of poetry heat? You wanted to feel the sensation of running, just once,
with the wrong crowd. Don't even think about it, if you know what's good.
I have bigger things still in my coat pocket—a ballad
that doesn't know when to quit, or an epic in heroic couplets
that would absolutely blow you away. So don't go somehow thinking
the world needs your heroics, too.

                        Now step away from this page, nice
and slow. There's no cause for alarm. You've stared down the dark
barrel of sawed-off inspiration long enough, and you're going to live
to tell about it. For all the good that does. As far as anyone else
is concerned, this whole thing never happened. It never really does.
Later, you can file a report with the glassy-eyed desk cop
or your local community college professor of English. They're not about
to put a stop to any of this senseless poetry violence.
They've been on the take for years, paid to look the other way.
They need the small-time, good-for-nothing hoodlum likes of me:
I'm their business, and that's not saying much,
but it's a modest living for us all.

                        I can promise you this:
it won't be long until I'm giving myself up to the authorities again,
to anyone who'll listen, and as usual they'll have no idea what
in the world I'm talking about. That's why I need you out there.
That's why I'm letting you go. I'm telling you, word for adamant word,
what I told you the last time: generally, I work alone, so this has to be
the end of the line, where we take one last deep breath together

before making our separate tracks back into the silence,
each of us imagining what we just got away with, at least
for another few minutes, in the middle of our unsuspected lives.

Belongings

It's one more wrong place to look if you really want something
for nothing. The woman at home in the easy chair makes it her business,
this assigning imaginary value to whatever flotsam
the world's washed up lately to her door. Some days it can't be
much of a living, but from attics and basements, forgotten
garages, from closets and cupboards and top dresser drawers,
from entire estates the recently departed have had to move beyond,
it keeps coming. And naturally it costs:

right this minute someone's negotiating a crawlspace
behind a small door in his life he'd all but forgotten, someone's packing
a box so full of the suddenly expendable in the puniest effort to make
room for anything he might find he desperately needs tomorrow
that he'll be breathing hard just trying to lift it, even *that* much.
He can't remember bargaining for any of this. His heart's not what it was.

And when eventually I pick up the slightest piece of it, someone else's
keepsake circuitously passed on to me, the weight of whatever history
feels like nothing in my hands.

■ ■ ■

I could let it go for a little less.

After all, someone's already had to. That's how it got this far.
She's learned never to be surprised: what people won't collect,
what people won't pay. She tries never to ask why. Take me:
at any moment I could be willing to go overboard one more time
for something at least as old as I am, hoping it's still in one honest piece
and working, if ever it was actually supposed to. Wondering
if it can be cleaned up, civilized, made ready for genteel society
again, can make it back home the long way from rust to shine.
That's always how transactions like this go:
the people on either end asking way too much to start with.

　　　■ ■ ■

How about if I ask what it's worth to you?

On the fairest days, the most reasonable weather the planet has
to offer, I'm here in the near-dark again, rooting through
yet another quaint-if-poorly-lit house or hovel of a storefront
trying to coax out just one iota more of the surely-finite treasure
sewn slapdash into this crazy-quilt world. I'm sweating into boxes
of stupefied toys, drawers rich in blotters and shapely fountain pens,
Atomic Age ashtrays and stacks of *Amazing Stories,* knowing all too well
the supply only seems inexhaustible. I've got my limits too.
And tired as I am of harummphing at the Precious, the hopelessly Pragmatic,
I'd still rather not walk out any door empty-handed, thanking her too
politely for nothing I can name, sure I've missed what should have belonged
to me, if only: a bauble's-worth of transformative whimsy I can't afford
to do without for life. I'd rather talk her down
to my no-account level, the level of so much of her hyphenated kingdom:

the worn-out, the broken-down, the cast-aside, stitched-
together, absolutely-caved-in and picked-over, helplessly
caught up in their own pathetic frenzy of collecting: dust and grime
that's been around, that's passed through innumerable hands
since the planet first began its particular, tenuous rearranging
and dripping wet, fresh out of the sea, people we'd hardly recognize
started hunting and gathering for all they were worth.

■ ■ ■

Everything's getting harder to find.

Until I'm home again with my latest peculiar rendition of
the so-little-it-takes-to-be-happy,
putting what once must have been a pretty good idea on the shelf
under the watchful photo portrait eyes of someone's durable family: perfect
thriftstore strangers. I've come to love them, their heroic smiles,
arms around each other as if they'd never be letting go:
the wool overcoat, the studded brooch, turn-of-the-century mail-order
fedora, slingshot, porcelain doll. They're smiling straight into the powder
and flash. Into the grainy future, and *poof:* they end up badly
framed, inexplicably here, part of the clutter of my suggestible heart
on display for anyone to see.

And although I'd like to believe that finally enough will be
enough, that sometime soon I'll be able to contain myself, a man
of moderation at last, I really can't imagine how.
So I guess what I could use most is a good talking-to, or else
more room to accommodate the thousands of small consolations
accumulating through the years: those days we actually do make it out of,
unbelievably intact. It's love, no matter how

eccentric, how impulsive, that undoes me every time. Love
for what's irresistibly, goofily human: some roughed-up, shopworn spirit
astoundingly imperfect, bought and sold in the blood
so many times since the first cell's splitting that whenever you *do* find it
it's usually hanging by the slenderest thread in genetic history.
I want to belong to exactly that kind of stubborn, crackpot joy.
That white elephant love requited, for now. Some days
I don't need anything more than that.

Nostradamus Had to Know

And this book full of mystery,
From Nostradamus' own very hand,
Is it not sufficient company?
        —*FAUST*, ACT I, SCENE I

I'm betting skinny Nostradamus must have taken it on the chin
more than once: that four-sided hat he sported wasn't big
on the 16th-century playground. It marked him as the bookish chump,
an easy shakedown for another day's bus money. Never once voted
Most Likely To Succeed, who could have predicted his enduring fame?
Eternal, sweet revenge on those who made him take the long walk home.
At first he thought his legacy might be the *Excellent & Most Useful*
Tract Of Everything Needed, For Those Who Wish To Become Familiar
With Many Choice Recipes—his celebrated doctor's-how-to-manual
of lozenges and lotions, powders and creams. But over 400 years later,
we mostly go to Wal-Mart for everything we need—although one diehard
living descendant still hawks a line of Nostradamus Jams & Jellies.

It's likely his parents never let up: *Be a doctor, Nostradamus.* And so
he enrolled in the first course required, Astrology, which meant something
half-respectable in those days: observing and measuring planets and stars—
a nascent form of Astronomy-still-on-the-horizon. Astrology's lesser half
assumed that every spinning body had been put in its heavenly place
for the benefit of the observer. And because this celestial display

was getting easier to predict, someone imagined the world of human events
should be equally foreseeable.

That's all Nostradamus needed to know.
The healing arts became less entrancing, paled by comparison
with staring into candlelight until the after-image burned in his eyes
and convinced him that, because it was nothing he could otherwise name,
what he was seeing had to be the future. And under the oblivious stars
he took to writing down his visions, always looking forward
to their circulation among the very rich, who'd spend some big French coin
for the services of a personal metaphysician.

He never once claimed
to know what any of his writings meant. From there it wasn't much
of a stretch—with no apparent talent, he still decided on a future
in poetry. And then he was off to the visionary races, sweating out
over 900 quatrains of events leading up to the planet's final days,
which diligent Nostradamians through the ages dated anywhere
from it-really-was-a-long-way-off 1999 to the safer boondocks of 3797.
When it comes to making sense of what's ahead, Nostradamus had to know
at least this much: there truly is no telling. And the book with anything
that never occurred to him before in his life—published as *The Centuries*—
has never been even for a moment out of print, never gone for long
out of occult favor. It's still brimming with abstractions of the always
popular natural disasters, wars, and political upheavals in no particular
chronological order. So much death and destruction by rampant metaphor—
the assiduously vague, the unflinchingly equivocal.

You'd think,
for all the heavy psychic lifting, Nostradamus finally could have named
some occasional names. Instead, that task has fallen to each
successive generation—filling in the yawning blanks, making the nondescript
shoe actually fit any one of history's conveniently recent footprints,
sized up wisely after the fact until it makes nothing but sense.

One editor who'd solicited new prophecies was dismayed:
Just got the two prognostications. I'm stupefied by your verbosity!
Today the fashion is to use fewer words. Those quatrains were nothing
like their attendant cover letter, composed in Nostradamus' naturally
sleek, meticulous prose. Maybe someone should have taken the prophet aside
and clued him in: Homer, Dante, and the Old Testament notwithstanding,
this dogged insistence on verse almost always ends badly—and not only
on the unforgiving playgrounds of the world after school. Generally speaking,
there's no real future in it. And I can see Nostradamus, undaunted
in his prescient wisdom, flashing his crooked schoolboy smile—yes,
but he has a certain gift where the future's involved: he's vigilant
in seeing to it that he has one. Now he's picking up his hat off the ground
again, placing it squarely on his head. He might not live to see it happen,
but it's just a matter of time until his makeshift star ascends
and takes its proper place, shimmering for all it's worth,
at the height of wishful thinking.

Criswell Predicts: Moon Landing or Not, the Usual Weekly Gathering of Friends at the Brown Derby—Los Angeles, July 20, 1969

Future generations from some other planet will dig through layers of rubble some
2,000 years hence. They will wonder what on earth was meant by the word
"Hollywood," and what in heaven's name was a Criswell?
   —FROM CRISWELL'S VISION OF THE END OF THE WORLD, FORESEEN AS
   AUGUST 18, 1999—HIS 92ND BIRTHDAY

That's him in the snappy tuxedo, the platinum-blond pompadour, the extra-dry
Beefeater martini marking his resplendent place at the head of the table
as always. He's lifetimes away from Indiana, from undertaker's son,
from his birth in the back of the family mortuary: *Jerrond Charles Criswell*
King. From ambulance jockey and quick-change morgue attendant. From high school
teacher and itinerant musician. From madcap newscaster, but oh, how
photogenic—and so, eventually to Hollywood, where he whimsically reinvented
his life as a colorfully off-center psychic. Where finally he's just Criswell—
small-talk of the town, a little bit of news himself.
                                        That's Maila Nurmi,
the once-popular-late-night-TV-horror-host Vampira,
James Dean's girlfriend near the end. Tor Johnson, who made a slight name
as pro wrestling's 400-pound *Swedish Angel,* then made the inescapable
low-budget movie rounds, landing roles that didn't call for too much English.
There's Ed Wood, who brought them all together for the first time
in his slaphappy *Plan 9 from Outer Space* a fortuitous thirteen years ago.
His buoyantly inept directing days have done their own slow fade,

and he'll never get anything close to the credit he deserves while he's still,
somehow, alive.

        For the moment, they're all oddly quiet, waiting for someone,
anyone, to walk on the moon.

        And Criswell's the unlikely celebrity glue
holding this played-out cast of characters together. Part of him believes
he could hang around a better class of Hollywood people, but Criswell's nothing
if not loyal to his friends. Whenever he wonders where he'd be without them,
that's always hard for him to say. He once caught the passing fancy of
Mae West, who gifted him with a Cadillac limo. But, hell: he's right here now,
isn't he? A ten-minute walk from home. More Beefeater in his immediate future.

The *Eagle* landed hours ago, and for the longest time they've just been
sitting there. At this table of tag-along celebrants, no one's making
any sudden moves either—not while Criswell's got them covered
with money to burn, inherited from the same spendthrift aunt who left him
two apartment buildings. He's been a Hollywood landlord for years,
so Criswell doesn't have to work too hard at anything.
It's been years since his TV show with the same name as his syndicated column:
Criswell Predicts. But like no other psychic before him or since,
he can still afford to be outrageously specific
to a fault—recently predicting the wholesale destruction of London by meteor,
cannibalism running wild in America's heartland, donor transplant organs
dispensed by vending machines, the overnight draining of Lake Michigan, and
of course: his not-just-any-psychic's-obligatory-stab at the end of the world.
His new book, *Criswell Predicts,* is making nearly honest money. An LP,
Criswell Predicts, is in the works, and next week he's booked again
on *The Tonight Show*—the clairvoyant who gave Carson his *Carnac* inspiration,
right down to the boffo sealed-envelope-pressed-to-the-forehead routine.
He's blazing a flamboyant trail for mass-media seers still to come—

from unctuous Uri Geller to Dionne Warwick's Psychic Friends.
These days he's worth his weight in small-time Tinseltown glitter.

This night is almost history already, although no one's walked out yet.
By now these best of liquored friends surely must be in each other's cups,
and they might not make it quite as far as those eventual, unsteady first steps
on the TV moon. Vampira's nearly drifted off the air for the night
when Criswell brings her back, whispering a not-so-secret message in her ear:
Can you believe there are idiots actually buying my book? Hell, I couldn't
look out the window and tell them what the weather's like. Ed Wood's thinking
what he could have done with NASA's budget-in-the-billions, how many pictures
he might have made with real stars. Tor is singing something in Swedish—a lullaby
or maybe a drinking song. No matter which, he can't help it: he'll be reduced
to a still-considerable mass of tears before it's over.

Criswell knows one thing for sure: the future seems clearer than ever.
And familiar, as if he's seen it before, pulling up the usual chair.
240,000 miles away, inside the *Eagle,* the astronauts are incredibly still
all talk. And from here, there is no simply turning back for anyone.
Two years from now the Swedish Angel makes his own ascent, taking
celestial wing. In nine years Ed Wood's heart goes suddenly wrong for good
after a lifetime of being only in the right place. Vampira's got two decades
before getting her small, retro due, suing America's new ghoul-next-door Elvira
for copping her camped-up horror-host act and getting away with millions.
And it's thirty nervous years until the doomsday that Criswell saved for the last
delirious page of his book:

> *So if you and I meet each other on the street that fateful day—August 18, 1999—*
> *and we chat about what we will do on the morrow, we will open our mouths to speak*
> *and no words will come out, for we have no future. You and I will suddenly run out*
> *of time.*

It turns out 1982's the unforeseeable year he'll walk smack into closing time
at his own private end of the world. He'll try asking for just one more
Beefeater martini, extra dry, but no one will be able to hear him.

For now, though, Criswell's still drinking heroically, still carrying on
with the less-than-solemn duties of his self-elected Brown Derby office.
He's lifting a glass, trying not to come across as anyone too impatient
for what's seemed like such a long time coming. It's bound to happen soon,
right before their astonished eyes—if only they don't pass out first
and end up missing it again—the latest half-assed momentous occasion
that promises somehow to change the way they look at the world forever.
Criswell's friends want to be there, either way, when it happens—not because
they believe too much in any kind of future to speak of, but because Criswell's
always been there, coming through for them again. He's gazing out the window
where the rain no one predicted is coming down like crazy, and he can't see
anything but stars in the sky over Hollywood, ever. He's so far off
from Indiana that he might as well be on the moon himself, where he's heard
there is no weather, good or bad, at all.

                          And he'll have to get going sometime—
under his own formidable power, no one on the ground, no Mission Control
to talk him through as much of the night as it takes him
to make his unheralded, extraordinary walk: a dozen blocks from here
until he's home again, and he can't wait. At least it's something
he really can see happening, say, from half a block away,
where unfailingly he'll pull out his gold-plated keys from his reliable tux.
And in his mind's mad dashing—through so much gin and rain
and history being made right then without him, through this staggering
final drop of the future that the night's not giving up completely—
he'll see himself, a man on a mission at last, unlocking everything.

Inside the *Eagle,* Waiting His Turn, Buzz Aldrin Can't Believe What He's Just Heard

Wow! Oh boy! Hot diggety dog! Yes sir!
> —ANCHORMAN WALTER CRONKITE, REPORTING NEIL ARMSTRONG'S
> HISTORY-MAKING FIRST STEP ON THE MOON

Did he just say *one small step for man?* I told him it had to be
for a *man*—or else that *mankind* bit seems absolutely senseless.
Any notion of symmetry and scale is shot to hell. To say nothing
of humility: the stepping, the leaping. The one guy, the many.
Like every gung-ho fly-boy, he's at his best in the air.
He's not used to saying much
that doesn't come out banged up on the ground. He made it
to the goddamn moon and, with some six hundred million people
watching on TV, he flubs the one line he couldn't stop rehearsing
all the way out here. These six hours since we landed, going
nowhere, gave him far too much time to dwell on his brief moment
in the reflected sun. He should have made up something entirely
new on the spot, when he could actually feel the gravity
of the situation—just one-sixth of any he'd ever known before.
Something lighter, maybe, when he could finally see
that first impressions here wouldn't carry too much weight.

I realize the name *Armstrong* has a ring that Buzz can't muster—
a certain all-American sonority that made him the obvious choice
to step down first into this staggering historical occasion. Yeah,

he got us to Tranquility by hand, overriding the onboard computer
when we were running scared and low on fuel, skirting an impossibly
rocky crash-landing, but still: I really should have put my foot down
before something like this happened. History has a way of forgetting
the kind of man who's second on the scene.

                                                          But this isn't exactly
the toughest act to follow. I can still be the first man on the moon
to walk and make grammatical sense at the same time.
Let Armstrong make the obligatory long-distance small talk with Nixon,
who's not about to miss out on his gratuitous piece of the action.
He'll come on the line with his self-important locker-room voice, insisting
we kicked some Russian butt out here tonight, unless—at the giddy
height of his power, and at least a few sheets to his favorite wind—
he ends up saying *some Russian's butt* instead. Which would make it
an even more limited triumph, but luckily nothing less than truly
the aim of this operation all along. And finally owning up to that much—
no matter who, or how imperfectly—would have to go down as one small step
in the right direction. But remember, even after I've struck what's left
of this lunar pay dirt myself: you didn't hear that, or even
anything close to that, from me.

Make Way for the Men of Science

Sure "the Big Bang" is a catchy phrase, but some astronomers think it conjures up the wrong idea of creation. So a stargazer's magazine is holding a contest to rename the birth of the universe. Entries may be sent on postcards only to Sky & Telescope's *"Big Bang Challenge."*
—AP WIRE STORY

When I told my poet friend in Wichita, he matter-of-factly said
Albert. After Einstein, maybe, which made some scientific sense.
Or after the cigar-toting alligator of endless schemes in *Pogo,*
so enamored of him is my friend. And of the comic world
he lived in once. After science or after art—anything but
after himself, of course: a name he's never been this sure of
in his life. And in his mind it's already settled, it's as good
as he can do, as good as done. As if it might be up in lights
before we're even finished talking.
                                            I thought he'd never ask:
for days I'd tried improving on the puny bravado of *Hey, You.*
On the vaguely ceremonious *Seat-of-the-Pants,*
if the actual beginning of the universe was anything at all
like what our worn-out piece of it lately's been flying by.

On certain starry nights I've been more optimistic:
Jasmine. Brandy. Crystal. Let's hear it for *Lili St. Cyr.*
For the constellations dancing overhead, shedding their exquisite
finery of light through one more dizzying late shift rotation.

And there's no way I can rule out the distinct possibility
of *Debbie Fuller,* third-grade angel who always made perfect
soap maps of the Americas, entire solar systems
out of hangers and styrofoam balls, who somehow loved me anyway
for my own theory of the universe: the Milky Ways, the Starbursts,
the Atomic Fireballs we could swear stretched out forever
in the semi-sweet darkness of Old Man Cooper's Five & Dime.

Or how about the sensitive, psychotherapeutic approach: what
does the universe want to be called? Something more relentlessly
19th-century, when you could almost count on *Patience* or *Grace*
or a little *Hope?* Don't we wish.

For my father, taking his time in the cosmic scheme, methodically
tearing down some celestial engine he won't ever put back together,
himself torn down to molecules and the infinite wisdom of space:
call it *Anything But Late To Supper.*

    ■ ■ ■

The Ford Motor Company went to a poet, inviting Marianne Moore
to name "a rather important new series of cars," admitting
the company's own ideas were, thus far, "characterized
by an embarrassing pedestrianism." I'm pretty sure:
no pun intended. She tried reading up seriously enough
on a world of "motors and turbines and recessed wheels."
And eventually she said *Anticipator. Thunder Crester. Silver
Sword.* She said *Turcotingo* and *Pastelogram.* And when she said
Utopian Turtletop, even Ford was somehow inspired
to send her two dozen roses, with regrets. But urging her on.
By the time she got to *The Intelligent Whale, The Resilient*

Bullet, and *Mongoose Civique,* she must have realized the Edsel
would never be anyone's idea of an automobile.

■ ■ ■

When I told my friend Albert there wouldn't be a prize
for the winning entry—except maybe the gratification of being
the creator of a new name for the scientifically accepted theory
that the universe began 10 billion to 20 billion years ago
when a single pinpoint commenced expanding into what we know
as all space, time, and matter—he said, "Then forget it."
It turns out at heart he's always been a Big Bang man anyway.

Maybe poets should stay out of things like this. They're in
over their heads every day as it is, and it's not easy coming up
out of sleep, back into the planet's fragile light, for air.
It's always some unnamed universe or other, arriving
in the borrowed clothes of death or love or the wrong kind of mail.
And it's not nearly often enough that roses show up at the door.

Now someone's calling for a few words on the debut of Everything,
the first rattle out of the cosmic box, sized to fit
on the back of a postcard. There used to be that wonderful time
we really could put everything we knew into a space that small.
And when we start missing those days, almost wishing they were here,
we're only kidding: they'd be as welcome as a carload of distant
relatives we barely remember having met.

I don't know if I'm prepared to meet the Big Bang Challenge.
I've dipped into relativity, the Unified Field,
gravity, black holes, and quarks. I've wrestled with anti-matter,

cleaned off my desk, made room to immortalize whatever occurs to me.
I've tried keeping a wide-open mind, but I can't help thinking

of Albert thinking of *Albert*. Now I'm up nights writing postcards:
Albert, Albert, Albert. Until it sounds as if I'm sighing
in his general direction again. But actually I'm stacking the deck
just in case, after all this dither, the winning card is chosen
at random. I'm doing what I can against astronomical odds.

Because there are worse names the cosmos could have to live with.
Because he's my friend. Because modesty prohibits me.
Because his name fits and still leaves a little room
to explain: we should all be so lucky. Just once.
Because Hurricane Albert blew itself out in a matter of days.
Because chances are slim he'll live on in the name of a gymnasium.
Because there's not a deli in New York that needs even one more
Celebrity Sandwich idea.
                            Because it's getting late.
And we've got a universe to think of.

(for Albert Goldbarth)

Short-Order Feng Shui

Because he's been attending weekend workshops in the Chinese art of placement,
my mailman has a lot to talk about these days. Soon he'll be moonlighting
as a professional feng shui consultant, so naturally he's already thinking
about me: *I want to be your real estate agent for the soul—location, location,
location.* And I say yes, but doesn't feng shui have a spiritual history
older than Taoism, older than Confucius? He doesn't really know about that,
but from the little he can see through my open door, he's in his own way
very concerned about my interior life: *You've got some chaotic* ch'i *in there.*
He tells me even inanimate objects are endowed with their own energy—*cosmic
breath,* if I will. And where I place them in relation to each other and myself
is particularly critical. Just yesterday he found out most of Hong Kong,
that international beacon of prosperity, has been designed in strict accordance
with the principles of feng shui.

 He wants only that kind of towering success
for me, that I might feel less pain wherever it's been building, might find
financial reward where it's never been before. He'd have me feeling luckier still
in love that doesn't quit. And while I admire that kind of attitude in a mailman,
I can't help worrying when he says he can't wait to *harmonize this house,*
smooth out the untold sharp corners, eliminate what he calls "the cutting ch'i"
that even as we speak is bombarding us with invisible, detrimental energy:
You ever wonder why there are no straight lines in nature? And I'm not sure
that's really true, but even if it is, I can't afford to lose my edge, not now,

so right away I'm spilling the rest of my feng shui guts, confessing the little
I didn't know I still had in me from college, where an aged Chinese calligrapher
shook his head over my feeble brush strokes, whispering all semester to me
that some arts are not for everyone. He could make that black ink dance like mad
across a field of rice paper in moonlight, but he professed not one grain of talent
for what had made his family back home famous down through generations—
feng shui, whose earliest practitioners were called upon as artists
to read the sacred signs and wonders of mountain, forest, wind, and water,
to articulate the most auspicious sites for villages, homes, even burial plots
where ancestors still could animate the breath of their living descendants.

Wow says the mailman, but in his eyes I see my story's already ancient history.
Right now he's more concerned that my bed might be on the wrong side of the room,
or worse—that the bedroom's never really been the bedroom after all.
That my lighting's too harsh or embarrassingly soft, and where, exactly,
do I put the myriad books and pop-culture paraphernalia he's been bringing me,
lo these many years? In his mind I am doubtless all over the place,
without even one truly comfortable chair. He knows so many ways to help me,

it's not funny. He's become an authorized dealer of wind chimes and bells—
time-honored enhancers of harmonious ch'i. He can supply all manner of pine cones,
driftwood, and rocks—the barely breathing detritus of nature. He's guessing
there's no room for an atrium right now, but I should at least consider a fish tank:
Every successful Chinese restaurant has an aquarium, you know, and against
my better judgment, I have to give him that. Now that we've harmoniously arrived
at this unusually mutual shred of understanding, we're both deciding he has to go
before he gets to the part about the salutary power of crystals. He's backing down
the uneven sidewalk, exhorting me: *That's way more than your front door—
it's your personal threshold!* He should only know about my threshold,
lower now than when this conversation started.

It mostly saddens me to see
one more venerable tradition so thoroughly sacked, co-opted by the spirit
of a New Age that seems to mean business—more genuine, practical wisdom reduced
to the practically ridiculous. But part of me is thinking what could it hurt, maybe
I should widen the footpath between my piles of Who-Killed-JFK books. Have the 1950s
Atomic Age ashtrays somehow turned into negative clutter, or do they still speak
energetically to me? Should my *Pogo* figurines stay put for the rest of their days,
knee-deep in the box of Guaranteed-Authentic Roswell Saucer Crash-Site Soil?
Do Charlie the Tuna hi-ball glasses work with Richard Nixon commemorative flatware?

I wouldn't know even how to begin revamping my chock-a-block life.
I have the perfect-fit love of a woman and the luxuriant son she brought,
across the only unmistakable threshold I can think of, into this world.
Living every day with them is my idea of harmonious arrangement.
So today I'm actually glad the mail he handed me is more mixed-up than usual:
I've got the next-door neighbors' Dylan concert tickets, a once-in-a-lifetime
sweepstakes come-on for a guy five blocks away, a postcard from someone's Aunt Ida,
who can't seem to get enough of the bed-and-breakfast life—so who knows quite
what exotica with my name on it is right now sitting in a stranger's vestibule,
its peculiar ch'i just waiting to be finally unleashed? It's a question

of credibility. Before he further insinuates himself into my house,
my feng shui mailman surely needs to put his own in order. Needs to get his mind
off the low end of higher things. He'll return tomorrow with his boundless energy,
ringing the bell, catching his cosmic breath if he can, ready to take it all back—
whatever he mistakenly delivered. He'll be here too long, poring piece by piece
through his copious bag, making sure I get every bit of what's coming to me
this time, and only that—going out of his way again to put things right
between the two of us. He sees me as the future prospect he can't afford to lose.
I hope this weekend's workshop breaks it to him gently, for both our sakes:
his future is the wrong place for the overcrowded, straight-line likes of me.

The Magician's Assistant Dreams of One Day Coming Clean

I was the volunteer from the audience who didn't know enough
to go back and sit down. When I saw what could be done with smoke and mirrors,
it turned into my whole life: learning precisely how to do my part,
how to take my humble share of the credit. I'm not about to give that away.
I'm in the complicity business: the ballet of intricate hardware, exquisite
misdirection and split-second timing. I'm in up to my neck
on the delicate illusion where the wall between what *seems* and what *is*
disappears in a moment where finally anything's possible. And it's too bad
some people won't let it go at that. They'd like a step-by-step explanation
of what it took to get there, as if in some way they'd be better off. As if
by magic, whatever they might foolishly imagine that to be.

Those mornings I wake up from another profound sleep I don't remember,
I put myself together, piece by unlikely piece. When no one's watching
I take a deep breath, and inexplicably I'm on the other side of my front door,
nearly invisible in a street full of people who've already taken the brightest
colors of the day and stuffed them into the wells of their clenched fists.
They'll go through the usual motions, the wishful patter,
and when they open their hands with that exaggerated flourish, chances are
they'll discover no shining coin, no lucky stone, nothing beyond the ordinary
desperate lines in the palm. The disbelief shows up
in their faces again and sure, they'd like to ask one more time how
there came to be so many knots in the rope the day tightens around them
that won't slip finally off. I would show them a little

something amazing if I could. It never seems to be enough just saying
how I've seen razor blades swallowed whole, one by one, then pulled back up
out of the darkness sized exactly to the shape of a man, and how
they emerged threaded together and gleaming: no longer a series of threats,
but a necklace, I promise, the strongest one ever.
Should the smallest thing go wrong, it's instantly apparent: the telltale
blood at the corners of a nearly unbelievable smile.

I know how it is: people in the thin air of their lives, spiritless
and floating through excruciating days while the gold hoop of everything
more than they ever could hope for passes over, under, all around them,
and what holds them up, what keeps them going is anybody's guess.
When they wake up disenchanted, visibly shaken, someone brings a glass of water
and just as they get it about to their lips, it vanishes
into the long history of things that never quite really happened.
And somewhere offstage in a private dressing room, death
like the uncle who didn't know when to quit when you were small, forever
yanking coins out of your ear with his two-bit hocus-pocus. He's dressed
in the cheap suit everyone remembers, practicing his smarmy show-biz kiss.
So far he's only brushed past them, picked their pockets, stolen them blind
or deaf or lame. But he's got them right where he wants them now: expecting
a slow cartoon bullet they can actually catch in their teeth.

There's not enough magic on the planet to turn every bruised face
into a sudden blush of flowers. There's no trap door waiting to be sprung
when the walls start closing in, no clever way out of the back rent
or the pills or the empty bed. No ingenious compartment, no secret
hiding place. Whenever we hit bottom, it rings unmistakably true.
They pulled a two-day-old baby out of a dumpster, scared
but alive, her pink nose quivering. A man races into a crowded church
because his voices told him to, and he knows what he has to do next.

Maybe he could have a little organ music, please: nothing up his sleeve
but a sawed-off shotgun and a *John 3:16* tattoo.
Every week another paycheck with someone's name on it goes up in smoke,
and it's never yet managed to reappear mysteriously in his other jacket,
in his ex-wife's dream, or in the paltry sandwich he'll choke down
on the job tomorrow while the foreman's off somewhere getting badly laid.

And the people who can't seem to get enough keep coming back
for more. They're volunteering everywhere, swearing the usual innocence: no,
we've never met before, there's been absolutely nothing arranged between us.
And whether we dress for the part in glittering sequins or the hand-me-downs
of a life much bigger than we are, whether somewhere there may be
doves on the wing or rabbits in the stew or luxurious silk handkerchiefs
in any pocket we choose, everything's too slight to wipe the sweat clear
off the brow, too soft to offer any meaningful resistance
when the world runs through the stacked deck of possibilities for today
and asks us to say *stop* whenever we so desire, as if it's somehow
in our power. And we haven't seen anything yet. No matter what
we'd like to believe. Later that night finds every one of us bent up
in the too-short box of sleep where the knives can't be much longer now.

I've been through that routine too many nights in towns all over,
in other clothes, under the different names hope goes by when it has to.
And in those darkened rooms where the magic words won't come, my heart
kicks in with some extra muscle. I've felt it rise to the occasion, ever
the assistant's assistant, holding up its professional end of the bargain:
keeping me together, letting me gently down, no matter how it has to
appear sometimes. Part of me's amazed when it works at all, when I make it
out of one more night alive. I know what's next: the sun, presumptuous
in the window. Like every wiseguy in the balcony so full of himself
he's overflowing, hollering *do it again.* He really wants to know how
I did it the first time, as if I could honestly remember back that far.

And instead of the classic assistant's decorum—polite smile and a bow,
the admiring glance across the stage at The Great Whoever it is this time
would still be elbow-deep in an empty top hat if not for me—just once
I'd like to yell out what I've learned about magic the hard way,
that too often it's whatever we've got left in the hat against the stinging
light of another inscrutable day the world throws shamelessly at us.
I don't know myself entirely how I've done it time and again, and surely
the world's not about to reveal itself completely. Magic is the art of
suggesting how much it's possible to get away with. Practice hard enough
and every passing minute will add to the irresistible life-
or-death ambiance a lot of people can't stop themselves from buying into.
Our job is making it look easy either way: whichever now-they-see-it,
now-they-don't effect we've decided to build a reputation on.

When tomorrow arrives tricked out with the linking rings of dread and wonder
like a necklace no one else could afford, I'll be there to handle them.
Each of us trying somehow to outdo the other in the simple act of
showing up, in doing even just that much again.

IV.

The World Doesn't End in New Jersey

I'll play it first and tell you what it is later.
—Miles Davis

In 1962 Redemption Was in the Air

and nothing like sweet woodsmoke from chimneys in a fairy tale.
In the story of our lives it smelled like overdone meat
on the grill of the neighborhood's unrelenting Mr. Bar-B-Q.
And long before I knew what deliverance was, surely I must have
prayed for it. I'd heard the word *redemption:* cross-legged
in front of a threadbare Sunday School flannelboard,
I squirmed my way through another love-of-Jesus lesson.
In those stories He always ended up dying
to save the future fledgling likes of me. The worried teacher
had her work cut out. The problem was making it stick.

I felt better about walking through the Valley of the Shadow
with WABC's Cousin Bruce Morrow cracking through each day's static
on my transistor radio—the only frill I ever talked my mother into
trading any stamps for. Cousin Brucie made a habit of preaching
the gospel according to Little Eva, to Bobby "Boris" Pickett.
So I did The Loco-Motion. I did The Monster Mash. It was easier
than doing The Only Begotten Son. The Everlasting Life. I believed
only in the wisdom of The Crystals' *just because he doesn't do what
everybody else does.*
                But I kept going along with my mother
on her annual pilgrimages to the local Green Stamp shrine—
a modest storefront showroom brimming with everything
she could ever want. She believed unflinchingly in that *S & H
Redemption Center* stencilled on the window in brilliant gold.

I'd help her lick the cheap glue on a year's worth of stamps
from supermarkets, filling stations, the occasional department store.
She'd known good Double Stamp Days, but her speciality was divining
when and where Triple Stamp Days were coming. And she'd be there,
loading up on anything she could think of that wouldn't go bad.
We pasted them into their flimsy books until she had more than enough
to turn another year of dreaming into the hopelessly pragmatic: cups
and saucers, throw rugs, a toaster, a set of wrenches she swore
my father could use. Every mother on the block loved the short-lived
feel of that sticky green assurance: something for nothing, at last.
Their apostolic fervor washed over me, of otherwise little faith.

My daily devotions were the bubblegum comics—Bazooka Joe
and his colorful pals, their carefree banter more than I could
hope to keep up with. But every kid I knew was in it for the fine-print
promises of *Free:* cap guns, badges, plastic submarines.
We'd find out the catch to this sugar-coated redemption:
it would take so many. And so long.
And we were so unwilling to admit that, yes, we had that
kind of time. Instead of the requisite 100 comics, I'd take
the hasty way out: *Or send 10 comics, along with a dollar.*
The Bazooka people were not about to lose their cartoon shirts.

I'd send in for everything at the mailbox on the way to school,
quietly singing along with Gene Chandler: *Nothing can stop me
now, 'cause I'm the Duke of Earl.* Wondering the whole day
when it would arrive and how long it would last—whatever I was
asking for now.
                    Every time the sirens went off we'd hit the floor,
crouching under our nutshell desks. The Triple Siren sent us all the way
down to the forbidding basement of Hamilton School, where we'd kneel

with our heads to the wall, hands over our ears—a version of prayer
the Supreme Court still allowed us—as if that was the only swaddling
we'd need to make it through. We'd learned to assume the position,
no matter how ridiculous. Between Kennedy and Khrushchev, we
didn't like our chances. How was their bluster about to redeem
our skinny grade school asses? We could barely manage the straightforward
maneuvers of a fire drill. No wonder Benny the Ball exploded one day
with B-movie eloquence I never saw coming: *We're getting ready for the end
of life as we know it.* His father had actually meant those words
as some consolation, digging madly for weeks in his own backyard.
Cousin Brucie played *Johnny Get Angry* after every day's 5:00 news.

None of us could help our puny selves. We understood so little
it was scary. This was someone else's fight, an overblown crisis
of faith and firepower, and we'd have to sweat it out again
in the red dirt of the playground, hoping whoever had the most to lose
would blink first, back off, eventually go home:
my mother, armed with her S & H stamp books, tenacious as any
true believer. Or the woman behind the Redemption Center counter
who'd just finished explaining that *no, this lamp is a floor model only.
I doubt we'll be getting any more in.* And my mother assumed
the worst—the position of righteousness. She'd come this far
from somewhere with no room for doubt. If she'd had a hammer,
she'd have hammered out danger. Hammered out a warning.
Next it would have to be love or the plate glass window.

When it came to Cuba, Khrushchev finally blinked. My mother blinked
and walked away with her stamps, her wounded pride refusing
to come unstuck completely. And maybe it was no coincidence
that our local Redemption Center closed its doors right after
the missiles were dismantled, hauled the long way back to Russia.

Now and then out of nowhere Benny the Ball and I would do
the Duck-and-Cover in the middle of arithmetic, but it never
saved us even once from any day's share of incalculable suffering.

My mother spent what was left of the year courageously
looking for the best in people again. Who knows where
she dug up her pieces of little-known news: if we collected enough
gum wrappers, empty cigarette packs, those new pull-tabs off cans
of soda and beer, the manufacturers would gladly take them back
and make a healthy donation to kids with special medical needs—
wheelchairs, iron lungs, seeing-eye dogs. Free time on dialysis machines.
There but for the grace of God, she'd say.
                                        And the entire neighborhood went
begging door to door for weeks, rooting through trash cans,
picking up the miserable slivers of anything
that reflected sunlight in the street—that is, until The Ball's father
set us pathetically straight. He wrote to Beechnut,
R. J. Reynolds, Coca-Cola. They wrote him back letters full of *this isn't
the first time. Don't ask us how the story. As much as we'd like.* And
sorry. Sorry. Sorry. As if that's what we had to be, too, for thinking
that holding onto a few of the sorriest pieces of ourselves
would be useful to anyone else, and the bad habits of a lifetime
could be reinvented as good news in a flash.
                                        We'd fallen for Redemption
As Ultimate Urban Folktale. We never seemed to get our fill
of The Phantom Hitchhiker or The Mouse in the Coke, even though
there's no catching up with the person it happened to, ever.
The DJ's spinning Elvis: *Return to sender. Address unknown.*
It's almost beyond comprehension: the person we meant to become.
No such number. No such zone.

I smoked pilfered cigarettes with Benny in the shelter
his father finally gave up on—he'd never dreamed salvation
could be so damn exhausting. He found it was less work buying into
one more inconceivable promise: the whole world would be breathing
a little easier now.
                        At first when we inhaled, we couldn't help choking,
but we would get to where we liked it. We had a plan in the unlikely
fantastic event that we turned out to be the last two people
this alive. We'd try to save our civilization the only way we knew.
Like those crumpled packs of Luckies we couldn't bring ourselves
to throw away: one small, glimmering, irredeemable piece at a time.
We'd *Twist & Shout.* We'd *Twist the Night Away.* We might even live
to *Twist Again, Like We Did Last Summer.*

And from somewhere down the block, the telltale smoke
of Mr. Bar-B-Q. When Benny yelled his usual *Stick
a fork in it, it's done,* we knew that wouldn't stop him. He'd never
concede that easily. We tried laughing, but those words would bounce
off the rooftops straight back at us—the most insidious fallout of all.
So we hunkered down, kept turning the future over
and over in our minds, thinking somehow we'd be able
to pull it out of the fire. We guessed we had it coming, one way
or the other. 1962 was almost done. We'd survived a year of alarming
possibilities that hadn't occurred to us before: we were accidents
or miracles still waiting to happen—John Glenn's Heroic Splashdown.
Marilyn Monroe's Crash-Landing. There was hardly anything
more we could hope for. We'd lasted this long
at our personal Ground Zeroes, and we felt strangely safe
in saying: if we had nothing but ourselves to redeem
for the rest of our lives, it wouldn't be the end of the world.

Going Wrong in the House of Neptune

The billowing cloth napkin still tucked into my collar
surely gave me away. I was a six-year-old in a hurry,
sailing into the wrong restroom in the middle of my family's
semiannual-flirtation-with-elegance Sunday dinner
at The House of Neptune Restaurant. I had to go bad, so
it barely occurred to me: this room full of women lining up
for their mysterious ablutions. They didn't seem real
horrified to find me, out of nowhere, among them—not even
a little annoyed. They continued talking softly, beautiful
in another language, laughing as if they couldn't possibly be
holding anything in. And my small urgency paled.

They were everywhere. On cushioned seats in front of mirrors.
Bowing over sinks where the fixtures gleamed like jewels
in some fantastic, untold realm. Those perfumes, lotions, and powders
knocked the young wind clean out of me: one more explorer
looking for a shorter route to the spices, blown off course,
stumbling into a New World he never bargained for,
so unfathomably exotic there's no going home even accidentally
the man he was—if there's any going home at all.

                                            I would know
soon enough: on my time-honored side of the bathroom story,
nothing's worth that kind of waiting for. I'd find myself
standing on the other side of that wall, trying hard

to take my rightful place in a row of men gazing straight ahead,
getting nowhere. We're clearing our throats, spitting if we have to,
listening for the slightest trickle of inspiration. If none comes
we hit the flusher anyway for show, careful not to say
a word, and walk away solemn, too full of ourselves.
An Ace comb once through the hair, and we're gone.

I needed those ladies-in-waiting to realize I'd made
an honest mistake. So there I was, owning up to a few puny things
I could be sure of: my name, my precarious and forgivable age,
everything I'd already had to eat, how many Cokes I'd downed
so far. For a moment it was the easiest I'd ever be among women.
When one of them winked and said *Sweetheart, why not
ask for a cherry in your soda next time,* I was painfully
aware of my ticklish position: old enough to be fascinated, but
too young for any lasting excitation. I wanted to crack wise,
or I wanted to kiss her and run. I wanted to piss
with the big dogs, whatever that exactly meant
I'd gone and done. I caught a glimpse of the future,
for what it was worth, the white slip showing underneath
her flowery dress. It was summer and salt air,
and The House of Neptune would never seem so enormous again.

I wanted to be remembered, to go down in history for being
the first to discover Something Big: a continent, an ocean
that changed the shape of the world forever. But I wasn't Columbus,
Balboa, or Vasco da Gama. I was just a kid in a seersucker suit
a long way from home, my whole life ahead of me
the only uncharted water I'd be crazy enough to wade through.
And maybe it was thinking of that, or the Cokes, or the waves
pounding the Jersey shore not far from the table window

where my parents were beginning to wonder, but suddenly what I felt was uncontainable. And I couldn't wait. I really really really really had to go.

Enough

Uncle Bud would always swear *they* had a pill
you could drop into the gas tank, and miraculously
you'd be talking 200 miles to the gallon, but no, *they*
were not about to let that out, that was something
he knew for sure. He'd read it in a magazine
and it turned into one of his favorite theories,
those flimsy sticks he rubbed together
trying to light up the dark *they* worked so hard to keep him in.
Sundays we passed the mashed potatoes around the table
for their pale, watery lesson: just when we think we can't
take any more, there we are in spite of it all, helping ourselves.

Bud loved dreaming up other people's secrets, letting us know
he was onto something big this time. It put a dollop of hope
into his hapless days: *they* breathed the same planet's air
as he did, and *they* had power, cigars, prestige to burn.
The one time I actually managed to whisper *enough's enough,*
I wasn't sure who I wanted to hear it: my uncle, my mother
in the relentless bounty of her kitchen. The inexplicable blue sky.
That's what they'd *like you to believe,* he told me, *so don't.*
And right before pie I stood corrected: *You'll find out too much
is not enough, not nearly, in this life.*

Each Sunday we watched him pull away
in his dilapidated Buick, looking incredibly

smaller behind the wheel than he'd seemed the week before.
No one wanted to tell me he was dying, that cancer cells
arranged his doing-in, at first a vicious rumor
slowly spreading, then turning more insidious and true.
He had to know the pain, if not the reason. No doctors
in cahoots would ever get their hooks in him, gladly
take too many days of his hard-knock salesman's money
for x-rays and needles and biopsy slides that only
might confirm what he'd secretly been feeling all along:
There's nothing we can do.

                        And I remember thinking:
if there truly is a pill, it would be only fair
to let him have it, finally, no questions asked. How much
could it hurt? And he wouldn't have to stop and ask
directions he never quite trusted. Or resign himself
to another three dollars of Regular and hope
he wouldn't run out before he made it halfway to anywhere.
In theory just this once he could drive himself crazy
or elated, unbelievably whole, and keep on going,
humming along with the steady engine—a secret at last
sized so exactly to his heart's desire that maybe he'd find himself
feeling like one of *them* for a minute, and for a minute more
at least, that would be enough. And having gone as far as he could—
almost off the map, falling into blue—maybe then
he'd really pull over, kick off his dependable shoes,
all in due time, forever.
                        And I knew it wouldn't be Uncle Bud
without one of the bad habits he couldn't break, swearing
his luck had changed into something more comfortable and good.
So I imagined him spitting into the ocean, still intent
on making his small difference, even in the face

of his own ridiculous dying: waiting out the dark, the rising tide, staking every one of his feverish claims all over again in the sand at the edge of the knowable world.

My Father's Less-Than-Celebrated Feud with Orson Welles

Incredible as it may seem, both the observations of science and the evidence of our eyes lead to the inescapable conclusion that those strange beings who landed in the Jersey farmlands tonight are the vanguard of an invading army from the planet Mars.

—FROM THE SO-CALLED "PANIC BROADCAST," ORSON WELLES
AND THE MERCURY THEATRE'S RADIO ADAPTATION OF H. G. WELLS'
WAR OF THE WORLDS

It went back to Grovers Mill, New Jersey, 1938, the night
before Halloween, when that first unlikely cylinder came down
and the Martians climbed out, rose up high on their metal tripods
and cut loose with those otherworldly heat rays on this Mischief Night
gone horribly wrong for the human race. Or so my father thought—
for a few hours longer than he liked to admit, even decades later.
When he first heard that Martians had landed a scant half-hour away
from his twice-mortgaged house in New Brunswick, he thought maybe this
would be the fiery end of the world. He'd never heard of H. G. Wells or
Orson Welles or the Mercury Theatre on the Air. But surely
no one would cut in on a live rendition of *Stardust*—Ramon Raquello
and his orchestra from the Meridian Room of the fabulous Park Plaza Hotel—
unless whatever breaking story was the kind that needed telling in a hurry.

And he couldn't wait to hear what on Earth was happening next.
The country had barely clambered out of the Depression
when the jitters over another world at war set in.

He lived by the radio in 1938, doing his best to keep up with Hitler
and Mussolini and Chamberlain on their way to the shaky Munich Pact, with
every one of FDR's smoky exhalations—*chats,* the President made a point
of calling them, although they were scripted, one-sided conversations.
My father retained an unwavering faith in what he called, simply, *the news*
in this storied year of the Lone Ranger, Snow White, and Superman.
The New York Yankee juggernaut had flattened the Cubs in four straight.
And my father stayed tuned to the radio. He listened to everything, hard,
trying to sort out the annual conflation of supposed villains and heroes.

■ ■ ■

And on that night, shortly after 8, all the free-floating fear in the air
came in for what felt like an unmistakably solid landing
outside a tiny farm town, *Pop. 200,* chosen at random
when scriptwriter Howard Koch closed his eyes and brought his pencil down
on the gas-station map spread out across his desk. And there, just barely,
was Grovers Mill, almost lost in the shadow of Princeton—an Ivy League town
my father always disparaged in his telltale workingman's way:
They think they're so smart in Princeton. But Grovers Mill,
and what was about to unfold, would never be quite so unheard of again.
For years after the broadcast, one enterprising farmer posted a sign: *50¢*
FOR A WALK THROUGH THE FIELD WHERE THOSE THINGS FROM OUTER SPACE CAME DOWN,
GUARANTEED! because such visits were rare and truly alien then, before
the postwar Age of Flying Saucers, before *The Day the Earth Stood Still,*
before the universal willies of Conspiracy and sinister Government Cover-up.
And for the rest of his life, my father would go miles out of his way
just to avoid Grovers Mill. Until Orson Welles,
he used to drive right through it, not even knowing it was there.

■ ■ ■

If only he'd been listening from the beginning, he wouldn't have missed
the announcer's introduction of "the director and star of these broadcasts,
Orson Welles." But he was switching from the rival *Chase and Sanborn Hour,*
where Edgar Bergen and Charlie McCarthy—the bright stars of Sunday night—
had just yielded the mike to some godawful singer my father had no time for.
He tuned in for the weekly antics, the cockeyed joy he never questioned:
a ventriloquist on radio.

                If only he'd hung on longer once he'd got there—
past the mock news bulletins, the on-location reporting that reminded him how,
by accident, he'd heard one of the first eyewitness news reports ever
when the *Hindenburg* caught fire over Lakehurst, New Jersey, the year before—
he would have found this havoc clearly staged, unleashed from a studio
on the twentieth floor of CBS, New York.

                    Or if he'd somehow thought
to change stations again, listening for what anyone else on the scene
was trying desperately to describe, he might have lucked back into
a triumphant dummy's latest wooden zinger or, less happily,
might have discovered Nelson Eddy nevertheless warbling away, and surely
he would have conceded: everything's still mostly right with the world.

Common sense would have suggested there wasn't time enough for this.
The creatures had left Mars, landed on Earth, deployed the invasion,
and completed the takeover in the unlikely space of forty-five minutes.
But common sense had been eclipsed by the darker, more exotic
power of Martian suggestion. And either way he looked at it,
the problem was real: everything was happening so goddamn fast.
My father could hear neighbors crying on their porches,
the sound of car horns, motors revving up and down the long block.

    ■ ■ ■

He never lost control entirely—a sinking feeling in his stomach,
yes, but he was not about to join the tumult in the streets.
He'd do his level best to stay cool, even under interplanetary fire.
Maybe he was thinking, seriously, if the Martians make it to New Brunswick,
he might not have to pay the butcher's bill. He was that determined
to be more or less himself—and damn the cataclysm.

                                                    At least he'd never be
the woman calling the bus-lines for information: *Please hurry.*
The world is coming to an end, and I have a lot to do.
He wasn't closing windows and turning out the lights
as if the Martians were distant relatives hitting town without warning
and could so easily be fooled into thinking no one's home. He wasn't
the preacher suddenly frozen in his holy tracks at the pulpit, and right now
he can't recall one comforting word from the Bible to save his life.

        ▪ ▪ ▪

He might have been able, one day, to pardon Orson Welles
for upsetting the delicate balance of a largely abstracted country,
but he could never forgive the finally undeniable fact that Welles
was only blowing smoke, making up the Martians as he went along.
And my father took personally anything that came through his 1938
state-of-the-art Zenith *Wave-Magnet.* He wanted so much
for just a small part of it to be real, the thrill of a little something
exotic going down in his lifetime, and he'd be there, in the thick of it
for once. He wanted an occasion he could rise to, anything
he could come out on the other side of, better off. And when that didn't
truly happen, he took it personally again. Not that he'd really wished
for the end of humanity but, if nothing else, how about
an actual Martian or two he could maybe lift a glass with on the porch,
raising himself—for one colorful night at least—out of the static,
the poor reception his heart's been getting lately.

And so he refused to go to any movie
that Orson Welles went on to make: no *Citizen Kane,* no *Journey
into Fear.* No *Touch of Evil* or *The Lady from Shanghai.* And when he heard
that a young hotshot Welles had scripted a few of the President's chats,
he had to turn his back on FDR. He turned off *I Love Lucy* in 1956
when Welles showed up as celebrity guest. And forget about the Hallmark
Hall of Fame's *The Man Who Came to Dinner*—not at my father's house.
Later, when Welles' star had fallen so low that he took the role
of TV pitchman for Paul Masson wines, my father would point at him
and say *Orson Welles, you are still an unbelievable horse's ass*
but, really, anyone could see he was still Orson Welles. And my father
was still my father, to that day not so much angry
as incredibly disappointed—as if the Martians, in staying so far away,
were giving him, and him alone, their entire planet's cold, red shoulder.

■ ■ ■

He saved the daily newspapers that came out in the wake of the broadcast.
He reveled in the way they were going after Welles with a vengeance,
never once acknowledging the self-righteousness of their crusade.
The newsbreaking power of stories in print had been preempted in a flash
by the electric immediacy of radio, and now the papers were only too glad
to expose "the perilous irresponsibilities" of the new
and instantly threatening medium: FCC TO INVESTIGATE RADIO DRAMA:
FAKE RADIO "WAR" STIRS TERROR THROUGHOUT UNITED STATES.

My father lifted them, yellowed and chipping, out of a box in his closet
as if handling unimpeachable state's evidence in the unending trial
of his century. And what he pulled out next astonished me:
a worn record album—"Never Before Released! Not a Single
Dramatic Word Cut! The Most Thrilling Drama Ever Broadcast on Radio!!!"
He handed it over so unassumingly on an otherwise unremarkable Sunday
nearly thirty years after the terrible fact of his disenchantment.
You can have it, he told me, and I thought maybe he was finally ready
to let it all go for good.

                     The war in Vietnam was heating up. LBJ
was sweating it out again on the living room television, but I hunkered down
next to the plastic record player in my upstairs bunker. I would try
to take myself back through my father's life to that night
his nutty and heroic grudge against Orson Welles began.
I set down the needle, closed my eyes, and prepared to become one at last
with a younger, more excitable, less complicated version of my father.

What I was hearing undeniably had its virtues, technically speaking,
but spinning around that far removed from its greater historical context,
it seemed slightly ridiculous to me—so many unsuspecting people
coming apart, no matter how short-lived their undoing. And secretly
I doubted it was anything I would have fallen for, ever.

■ ■ ■

The lawsuits brought against CBS, the Mercury Theatre and, yes,
against Orson Welles himself, amounted to over a million 1938 dollars
for broken legs, bent fenders, miscarriages, lost wages, and untold
psychic damage. With no obvious precedent on the books
for determining genuine liability, none was ever amply substantiated.
But against the advice of company lawyers, one claim was actually settled—
a handwritten note that said:

> *I thought the best thing to do was go away. So I took $3.25 out of my savings and bought a ticket. After I'd gone sixty miles, I knew it was a play. Now I don't have money left for the shoes I was saving up for. Would you please have someone send me a pair of black shoes, size 9-B!*

And Orson Welles himself sent them out in the next day's mail.

■ ■ ■

For years, the beleaguered citizens in the vicinity of Grovers Mill
preferred not to talk about 1938. Some were vaguely embarrassed,
and the rest were more than fed up with the lingering
sociological attention. But with the fiftieth anniversary looming,
things changed dramatically. The sons and daughters of the sick-and-tired
formed a War of the Worlds Committee. They staged a four-day celebration
featuring lectures by authentic Princeton astronomers this time,
a Martian costume contest, a dinner dance under the cool October sky
where a local high school band knocked out the ever-popular *Stardust*
before taking its best shot at *Flying Purple People Eater.*
Howard Koch was guest of honor at a full-blown reading of his radio script,
although the last half-century had caught up with him, and he begged off
taking part in the subsequent Martian Panic 10K Run.
People came unabashedly to embrace their unique station in cultural history:
one of the only places on Earth at least a little famous
for what never really happened there.

                             And if my father had been still alive
in 1988, this really might have killed him. No one could have paid him enough
to show up, although I don't think the War of the Worlds Committee ever
would have given him their serious consideration. They'd been hoping for
Orson Welles, who surely would have come if they'd offered him enough,
and if he hadn't been three years dead himself. Instead, they issued
a spirited proclamation naming Welles an honorary city father. And since I
was the only one of the three of us still alive, it must have been me
saying out loud over morning coffee, over the further droning of the radio,
that figures—in honor of my father, that distinctly un-Orson Welles, even
anti-Orson Welles, who was still my only father. I was hoping that—
because I'd finally spoken up, for once taken his side in the eternal struggle
against his nemesis—maybe now he'd actually stop talking in my sleep.

■ ■ ■

The last time I was in New Jersey, I drove through Grovers Mill.
I saw the monstrous water tower standing tall on rusted metal legs,
still pockmarked from that night in 1938
when local farmers armed with shotguns roamed the countryside
in the unfathomable dark, looking for no-account Martians to bring down.
I found a modest marker: *Historic Site of the Martian Invasion*,
erected by the civic-minded War of the Worlds Committee, who apparently
didn't believe that *Historic Site of My Father's Wishful Thinking*
had quite the resonance they were looking for.

I drove north along the Millstone River, half an hour at most, until
I arrived at the more familiar marker with my father's name and dates.
I stood there for a while, trying to think only of the good that came
from his compelling lifelong feud with Orson Welles, from his solemn vow
to never again be taken in so absolutely or to have his spirits lifted
so impossibly high. From that disconcerting night forward,
whatever the latest hard-luck wrinkle in his life or anyone else's,
he'd get this nearly wistful look on his face right before conveying
his hard-won assurance—the expression he came to be locally famous for:
It's not the end of the world. I was only a little surprised
that it hadn't shown up on his headstone—one last time, for the ages.

I remember him breaking the news to me when I discovered one of his heroes
for myself: no matter how often the story gets told, in fact there's nothing
even remotely like *I'd rather be in Philadelphia* at the grave of W. C. Fields—
my father's comedy god and frequent Sunday night guest blowhard adversary
of Charlie McCarthy, America's favorite dummy. Millions of listeners
could cite chapter and verse, every sidesplitting putdown
in their celebrated feud.
                              It's not the end of the world, he said, noting
my obvious disappointment. But what good were any of the words we lived by
if it turns out they were never really carved in stone?

In his heart there seemed to be nothing he hadn't heard before—
he'd been to the end of the world as he knew it, and he'd spend
the rest of his life trying to make it mostly back, carrying with him
the dead weight of that astonishing Martian no-show. I wanted to say
at last I understood why he could never let it go. But I didn't.
I still couldn't imagine walking those last forty years in his shoes.
Maybe Orson Welles would have tried to do right by my father, too,
if he'd had even an inkling of this egregious and longstanding wrong—
and then if only he'd known exactly what kind of apology
my father might have been persuaded, finally, to try on for size.

■ ■ ■

The same man who never found it in himself to forgive Orson Welles
always managed to forgive me so completely, it was frightening.
Every one of my effortless childhood transgressions, promises like so many
broken windows, the bad-necktie gifts I repeatedly signed off on,
the dents I put in his beloved Chevrolet on the Edison Diner parking lot,
where it was invariably half-past bar-time: *It's not the end of the world.*
Even when I couldn't stop myself from watching—in the sanctity
of his own living room, on his first-ever color TV—George Pal's 1953
War of the Worlds five nights in a row on Million Dollar Movie
(this time the Martians arrived in California, buzzed around in genuine
flying saucers, and were subsequently A-bombed, and Orson Welles
had nothing to do with that): *It's not the end of the world.*
This was his generous absolution, and more—his grudging lifetime
guarantee that even when things fell short of the best anyone could hope for,
believe him, they could always be worse, no matter how unthinkable that was
as I pondered the inscrutable arithmetic of high school. Add to that
the goggle-eyed mysteries of shop class. Take away Debbie Fuller, lost
to her family's inexcusable decision to leave town.

                              Whatever happened
to that moony girl you were sweet on? and I wasn't about to say
Princeton, because without a doubt that would have got him going, and
for nothing. For all I saw of her again, it might as well have been Mars.

    ∎ ∎ ∎

Here is where, at last, it has to end—where enough will finally
be enough: this oddball song of abiding love for someone who became
convinced he was a different man after 1938. And his unrequited feud
with the person he so tenaciously held responsible. This is the end
all good things must come to, for better or for worse.

So take this,
Orson Welles: in the name of the father and the son who survived him,
you are here forgiven. And Howard Koch, who gave back the world
in *Casablanca,* four quick years after masterminding its destruction:
forgiven. For FDR, a newer, better deal on his place in history than the one
he ultimately got from my father. This is for the Martians, who fell
short of my father's expectations, who chose to stay home, wanting nothing
really to do with humankind. For the small towns scarcely on anyone's map
and the people who think they can leave them behind on their frantic way
to somewhere else. For Debbie Fuller: I have to admit that it wasn't
the end of the world. This is for the ghostly world of all our fathers,
so far now beyond the pale that they can't be bothered anymore—

but especially for my father, younger than I ever knew him, before
the Great Disheartening: the Sunday comics pages are still unfolded
on the kitchen table. In the kaleidoscopic desert of Coconino County,
Krazy Kat gets beaned on the noggin by another sure-fire Ignatz brick
and keeps on singing just the same, strangely more in love than ever.
And Buck Rogers is cruising his colorful 25th Century, coming to the last-
minute rescue in his super-autogyrospectomoscope. But that's 500 years away.
And my father's still sitting close to his spiffy, dependable Zenith,
still laughing at Bergen and McCarthy until it hurts, because
there's so much going on already in the world that's nothing to laugh at—
and he's not about to change the station this time.